The
Wo...s
Ha...k

GW00492891

Choosing, installing and
operating your stove

First published in Great Britain 2013 by

Posthouse Publishing,

The Old Post Office,

Swanton Novers,

Melton Constable,

Norfolk, NR24 2AJ

www.posthousepublishing.com

A CIP catalogue for this book is available from the British Library
ISBN 978 1 903872 32 1

A catalogue record for this book is available from the British Library.

Printed in Great Britain

**Publishers acknowledgements**
The publishers would like to thank Sune and John Nightingale of Stovesonline for
their invaluable help in the compiling of this book and for supplying a large number
of the images. The publishers would also like to thank all those stove manufacturers
and distributors who also kindly supplied images.

# Contents

# Introduction

Thirty years ago the woodburning stove was the cast-iron behemoth that put the Aga into aga saga and whose habitat was a farmhouse-style kitchen in a 17th-century manor-house in the Cotswolds. It's come a long way since then!

Today, woodburning stoves are more popular than ever, spreading the same cosy warmth and cheery glow throughout the lounge as an open coal fire but much more efficiently and with none of the mess. That they're completely carbon-neutral pleases many of the people who install them. But opting for a woodburner doesn't mean compromising on style. Yes, you can still have the kitchen range complete with hob, oven, and back-boiler if that's what you dream of; you can even integrate it with solar panels to create a single system that cooks, heats, and fills the radiators all year round. But stove design and technology have evolved so rapidly that you could opt instead for a slim, discreet, elegant model perfect for the most minimalist of white cubes.

Whichever end of the continuum you prefer to inhabit, you'll find your woodburner will soon become more than just a heating system. It's nothing like a gas boiler that you simply turn on or off or leave on timed. Selecting the model that suits your needs calls for specialist knowledge and expert advice. The installation itself generally requires official approval. And once installed, even the most technologically advanced design – a modern marvel of fuel efficiency and temperature control – needs a modicum of maintenance and management. Then there's the wood itself: you can simply have your logs, briquettes, or pellets delivered regularly; or you can stray into the whole delightful world of small woodland management, growing, managing, felling, seasoning and splitting your own trees.

However deeply you delve into your woodburner's potential, one thing's for sure: you won't take it for granted. Treat it well, pamper it, flatter it a bit and it will soon be more of a household pet than a household appliance. But as with any pet, it needs a certain amount of practical knowledge if you're to get the best out of it – and this book is the ultimate guide for anyone thinking of choosing a wood-burning stove. **Chapter One** explores the fantastic variety of models and styles on the market and examines the technological advances that have made woodburning stoves the most fuel-efficient and environmentally friendly way there is to heat your home. **Chapter Two** goes into the complexities of installing a woodburner from building regulations to the importance of lining your chimney, and has a host of links to sites that will tell you who to contact for advice. **Chapter Three** is all about the stuff at the heart of it all – wood. **Chapter Four** includes a directory of stove manufacturers and distributors which guides you towards the size and type of stove that's right for you.

## Publishers Note

The publishers and the editors of this book have made every attempt to ensure that the information contained is as accurate and as up to date as possible. However stove manufacturers are constantly changing their product ranges and our advice is that you should always consult your local dealer before making a final decision.

Throughout the book the editors have recommended that you use a professional installer for all stove installations. The publishers highly recommend that you consult HETAS website **www.hetas.co.uk** where a list of their approved appliances, retailers, installers and chimney sweeps can be found.

# Chapter One
## Which type of stove?

◀  An Arkiane Kephren stove.

## Which type of stove?

With the prices for oil, gas and electricity continuing to rise and speculation that demand will soon outstrip supplies, the sale of wood stoves has risen enormously. Wood has the advantage of being a very low carbon, sustainable fuel that can often be sourced locally. Modern stoves are efficient, come in many sizes and styles and, if you have a boiler stove, can also provide your hot water and central heating.

Following a short history of stoves and how modern examples evolved, we explain the various parts of a stove and introduce some of the technical jargon you are likely to come across. We then look at the various types of stove available, how to pick the right one for you, and cover a variety of related subjects along the way.

The simplest way to burn wood is to make a bonfire, the method our ancestors began with. One can imagine that with the wind blowing they noticed that piling up some stones and earth around the fire helped. Building up the sides of the fire and creating a channel for air to enter further improved and concentrated the heat for cooking. Over time the simple bonfire became more and more enclosed giving greater control over the temperature of the fire, the air supply to it and the path the hot gases took to escape.

Throughout the world there are still many people who use open fires for cooking. These are often made from earth and have one or more openings at the top for pans to sit on and an opening at the side to feed the fire with wood. These simple fires often lack a chimney so, if used indoors, can fill a room with smoke causing eye, respiratory and other health problems. Adding a simple chimney or flue (a tube to carry the smoke outside) can reduce or eliminate these health risks. Adding a door so that it is easier to regulate the air supply will also make it more controllable, use less fuel and make cooking easier.

## Fireplaces and open fires

The UK has had a long tradition and love affair with open fireplaces. Many people still ask if they can burn their stove with the

▲ A distinctly English inglenook fireplace. While the fire looks great and probably feels warm, it will do little to heat the house and will cool the house down when not in use.

doors open so that they can hear the crackling of the fire and 'get really hot'. Paradoxically the stove will actually give out less heat with the doors open than if they are closed as more air is drawn through the wide opening.

Placed centrally in the building, historically the fireplace was a simple large opening in a masonry wall with the chimney built above to draw the smoke up and away. From the Rumford fireplace designed by Sir Benjamin Thompson in the 1790s, many improvements have been made over the years leading to the familiar small coal-burning fireplaces so often found in Victorian town houses. Because a fireplace is a large opening connected to the atmosphere by a chimney or flue, large amounts of often warmed air are sucked up to the outside world. That air has to come from somewhere and so an equal volume of colder air is sucked into the house through any available opening. Depending on its design, the efficiency of an open fire can vary dramatically.

When a fireplace is not in use, lots of the nice warm air inside your

This coal fired antique cast-iron range cooker was made in Kingsbridge, Devon, and was designed to be built into a wall.

A tall, antique, cast-iron stove from Denmark. Some of the designs were twice as tall and featured intricate crowns and patterns. These stoves were very efficient at burning coal but not as good as burning wood because of the small firebox.

A cast-iron range cooker from the USA which was made in the early 1900s. The stove was known as the Hay Burner and did just that; bales of hay were fed into the stove on the right hand side and the spring mechanism slowly pushed the bale into the firebox.

house is still being sucked up through the chimney to the outside. In some cases it may be a sensible idea to block off the chimney in some way when your fire is not alight. A metal plate that can be opened and closed is an option where the fire is used intermittently. Where a fireplace is no longer in use it is important to provide ventilation holes at the top and bottom to allow some air flow to keep the chimney dry.

And remember that while an open fireplace is sucking air out of your home, the air replacing it is fresh aire which can help to ventilate the house.

## Some stove history

As the open fire was steadily improved by banking earth, rocks and clay up around it, it's easy to see how the masonry stove developed especially as the materials were readily available and easy to work with. Examples of masonry stoves from the 18th century still exist and they were being made well before then. Masonry stoves soak up or absorb the heat from the fire into the material they are made of and then gently release this stored heat into the house, often for some time after the fire has gone out. Some consider this a step up from simply passing the heat straight to the room, although there may only be limited control over how quickly a masonry stove releases the stored heat back into the home. The alternative to this is to use the boiler stove to heat a large volume of water which can be stored for later use.

Some North European masonry stoves are huge with long and convoluted flue pathways to extract as much heat as possible from the fire. Some are so large that you have to light a fire at the bottom of the chimney to heat it up and get it drawing well enough to be able to light the main fire. A masonry stove like this can be very efficient but, because of its size, requires a lot of space and is probably better designed into a house as it is being built.

Cast iron stoves were being made in Denmark in the 1640's. Then later, with the adventof the industrial revolution and Abraham Darby's patented cast iron manufacturing techniques, they really took off.

Coal, seen by many as the driving force of the industrial revolution, was plentiful; it smelted the iron in the furnaces and was the obvious choice of fuel for these new metal stoves. In the UK particularly there is also a long history of cast-iron coal burning range cookers that form the heart of the kitchen and are often kept alight 24hrs a day.

There are some very ornate stove and cooker designs from the 19th century, some freestanding models and others designed to be built into the wall of the chimney breast. Of the built-in versions, the surrounding walls often formed part of the overall structure with some even using multiple flues built into the wall to make optimum use of the flue gases. The flue gases could be directed to a particular pathway depending on whether you wanted to heat a hotplate or oven.

Freestanding room heaters became more and more popular with Scandinavian stoves of the period adopting a tall and cylindrical design. Such was the thickness of the cast iron that many of these stoves survive to this day. The time, effort and detail that went into the castings were remarkable, often featuring delicate figures, flowers and patterns around doors and the case of the stove. Often made in parts that would slot or bolt together, the skill of the pattern makers was self evident when working with a material that would shrink by around an eighth when cooling down in the mould.

## The Clean Air Act, smoke control areas, Defra exempt stoves

In the early to mid 20th century with coal the dominant fuel for domestic stoves, it was also being used in enormous quantities to drive industry and generate electricity. Air quality in major cities and industrial areas started to suffer and, when the combustion products from coal burning combined with poor weather and fog, the resultant dense smog was disruptive and life threatening.

In London in 1952 'the Great Smog' was said to have claimed the lives of around 4,000 people and the government introduced legislation to combat and attempt to eliminate the problem. In 1956 the first Clean Air Act was introduced, which gave local authorities the powers to control smoke emissions and to introduce smoke control areas. This was followed in 1968 by an amended act with more stringent 'clean air' requirements as it became clear that the deaths in 1952 were grossly understated. It is now thought that there may have been as many as 12,000 deaths directly related to the Great Smog.

Smoke control areas are still in force today and cover most of our cities and major towns. Within these areas it is illegal to burn coal, wood or any other fuel unless the stove and or the fuel have been tested and exempted by Defra, the Department for Environment, Food and Rural Affairs.

You can check if you live in a smoke control area and which stoves you may be able to use by visiting **www.uksmokecontrolareas.co.uk**. If you live it a smoke control area and have any doubts at all about what type of stove you can use and what types of fuel you can burn, contact the environmental health or building control department of your local authority for further information.

Defra exempt stoves have been tested and approved for use in smoke control areas because they have high efficiencies, low particulate emissions and the air supply to the fire cannot be completely shut off. Essentially this ensures the fire always carries on burning properly if there is fuel left to burn. We will look at how the firebox in a stove works a little later.

Sometimes called slow or slumber burning, overnight burning is one of the least efficient ways to burn any fuel. Usually achieved by reducing the air supply to the fire, the resultant combustion is less complete than normal and can result in an increase of particulate emissions.

Even if you do not live in a smoke control area choosing an efficient stove with low particulate emissions is a good idea as you will use less fuel and minimise your contribution to atmospheric pollution.

More and more stoves have been added to the Defra exempt list in recent years, many of which are suitable for burning wood in smoke control areas and are clearly marked in the 'product directory' featured later in this book.

So the good news is that, with very few exceptions, it no longer matters where you live if you wish to enjoy the comfort and heat produced by a wood burning stove.

## Coal falls from its pedestal

For twenty years from the late 1940s, gas as a domestic fuel was heavily promoted and the way in which it was sold improved. In the 1960s the UK converted from coal based 'town' gas to 'natural' gas, which came directly from underground reserves in the North Sea. With the introduction of natural gas, coal rapidly lost its foothold and stoves all over the UK were decommissioned, to be replaced by more convenient gas fired boilers and cookers.

Gas, like coal previously, was viewed as a virtually unlimited fuel source and, despite recent price rises, is still relatively cheap.

However there is growing awareness that supplies of all fossil fuels, which we are consuming at a prodigious rate, are limited. With the rest of the world starting to wake up to its own version of the industrial revolution, oil and gas supplies are in ever greater demand with some suggesting that we are now using oil and gas at the fastest rate ever. This is one of the greatest arguments for heating with wood.

Wood sourced from properly managed forests is a renewable and sustainable fuel. Although it is not possible for everyone in the country to heat their home with wood as there simply is not enough (and wood has many other uses), there are still vast reserves of wood in our forests and every year we dispose of millions of tonnes of 'waste' wood, which could arguably be put to better use.

## The alternative resurgence

The 1960s and 70s saw a small resurgence in UK stove sales driven in part by a group some described as the 'alternative movement'. These people saw the good sense in reducing consumption and increasing sustainability, terms that have since become widely known and are nowadays key phrases in the media.

Wood was and is a sustainable material to use for heating and also perhaps appeals to those who wish to be that bit more independent

◄ TOP RIGHT: A cast-iron Morso 1442 Defra exempt stove – a perfect size for a living room.
◄ TO LEFT: A Defra exempt Firefox 5 is great value for money.
◄ A Defra exempt Franco Belge Savoy Mk 2 with smoke control kit fitted.

and self sufficient. The alternative movement promoted ideas like sustainability and organic food, not popular subjects at the time, with many thinking their advocates were at best odd or at worst mad.

During the 20th century stove manufacturers had been moving to smaller models. In Scandinavia the traditional tall cylindrical models grew shorter, and in the UK the box shaped stove became the norm. Losing the height of the stove meant that there was a shorter path for the flue gases to travel and less time to extract the heat from the fire before it was lost up the chimney. Since these first 'lower' stoves were introduced, improvements have been made to return to the efficiencies of the earlier taller models by introducing baffle systems within the stove to lengthen the path the flue gases take before being released up the chimney.

## Contemporary stoves

Paradoxically the tall cylindrical style stove has been making a come-back with many of the latest models originating from Scandinavia and particularly Denmark. As earlier, the taller body shape means that the flue gases can be made to travel further before passing into the chimney thus extracting more heat and generally leading to higher efficiencies. Although overall efficiency depends on a number of factors, these tall cylindrical stoves are often well over 75% efficient with some models now even more efficient. Further design improvements may one day result in efficiencies of over 90% although it must not be forgotten that as the efficiency increases, the amount of heat passing into the chimney reduces. As the efficiency increases, the design of the chimney and flueing system becomes ever more important as, we will explain in more detail later.

Unlike many of their predecessors, contemporary stoves feature large windows to provide a view of the burning wood. Some models even provide views from three sides. Major advances in the materials used for the windows has resulted in high temperature shatter-proof 'glass' that can withstand the constant cycling between high and low

▶ A Westfire 33, showing the trend for making taller stoves again.

▲ **TOP** The La Nordica Fortuna Panorama not only has wide curved glass in the main door, but two extra slit windows to each side of the door give an extra wide view of the flames.

▲ **BOTTOM** The Panoramic FX 1 from UK manufacturer Future Fires has one of the widest fully curved windows around.

▶ **RIGHT** A Charnwood Pico .

temperatures, is easy to keep clean and will not normally need replacing in the life of a modern stove. A word of caution. The glass used in modern stoves is not window glass or anything like it so do not be tempted to replace it with anything other than the correct material.

## Parts of the stove

**Air-wash** Most modern stoves have what is called air-wash a technique first exhibited by the UK stove manufacturer Arada. Air is blown over the window of the stove in a sheet. Often the air comes from above the window and is supplied through a long slot at the top of the window. Sometimes air-wash is also supplied at the bottom of the window. Often the air for the air-wash is preheated by running it through ducts in the body of the stove.

Tars and other deposits from the fire condense when they cool and can accumulate on any cool parts of the stove. This particularly occurs when the stove is first lit, being refueled or burnt very slowly. The window in the stove is often cooler than the rest of the firebox and is the one place where any tar deposited will be readily visible. Air-wash reduces the tarring on the window by physically keeping the gases away from the glass, although some tarring is inevitable. Running the stove in its highest heat mode for a short period will often burn off the tar, but remember that a stove window that keeps

▲ Firebricks protect the body of the stove from the very high temperatures found in the firebox. Firebricks can be made from hard cast bricks, or from softer vermiculite board.

▲ This is a circular grate from a Morso stove. It can be riddled by using a handle which lets you turn the grate back and forth.

# The Parts of the Stove

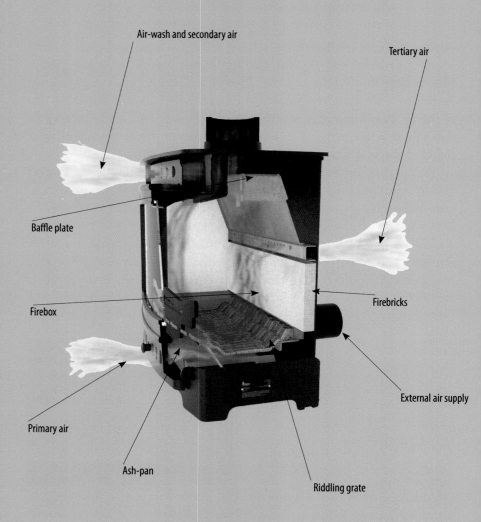

Air-wash and secondary air

Tertiary air

Baffle plate

Firebox

Firebricks

Primary air

External air supply

Ash-pan

Riddling grate

▲ A Villager stove from Arada showing the various parts of the stove along with relevant air supply sources.

going black could be an indication of other problems and is often associated with burning 'wet' wood.

Air-wash may also function as the source of secondary air to the firebox. Many modern stoves have some air-wash on all the time, and you cannot turn them right down. That means that the window will stay clearer longer and the stove will run more efficiently and produce less smoke.

Ash pan Some wood burning stoves have an ash-pan under the grate. The role of the ash-pan is pretty obvious: to contain ash and make it easier to take away from the stove. An ash pan will usually have a handle, which allows you to pick it up using the tool provided with the stove, though do remember that the ash pan and the ashes in it are often very hot. It is a good idea to have a galvanised bucket into which you can empty the ashes from the ash pan The ashes cool in the bucket and can then be disposed of later. Wood ash is fine to put on your garden or in your compost. Ash from coal should not be used like this. In many modern wood burning stoves the ash pan has reduced in size and is really there to provide a method of routing and controlling the primary air supply below the grate.

Baffle plate The baffle plate is usually made from metal but increasingly highly insulating vermiculite baffle plates are being used. The baffle plate rests above the fire, usually at the back of the firebox at a slight angle, blanking off the direct path to the flue exit of the stove. The hot gases from the fire have to travel around the plate to get out to the flue exit. As they travel around it the heat from them passes to the metal case of the stove and can then be convected out to the room so you can feel the heat. Some stoves have more extensive baffle systems, or a series of baffles to make the path taken by the hot flue gases even longer so as to extract more heat from them. Chimney suction is referred to as draw or draught. The draw from the chimney is what provides the suction needed to move air through the stove. Modern, heavily baffled, stoves also route the air to the firebox very circuitously and so a stronger suction is needed to make the stove work well. A well insulated chimney is essential to make the stove draw well.

**Chimney draw or draught** Chimney suction is referred to as draw or draught. The draw from the chimney is what provides the suction needed to move air through the stove. Modern, heavily baffled, stoves need a stronger draw to make the stove work well. A well insulated chimney will generally help to provide a strong and consistent draw.

**External air supply** Stoves are now being made with the ability to connect to an external air supply. Being able to use an external air supply may become essential as our houses become more and more airtight.

Your stove needs air to work so if it comes from the room in which the stove is located, you may require an air vent directly into the room itself. Although opening up a hole in the outside wall to admit air sounds rather drastic, there are many through the wall ventilation kits available that will minimise the potential for draughts. Using an external air supply eliminates the potential for draughts in the room.

Some stoves have the ability to connect just the primary air to an external air supply, others have the ability for all the combustion air to be supplied via the external duct.

Current UK building regulations mean that an air supply to the room is also required even when a direct air supply is fitted, the argument being that air is needed from the room when the stove door is open.

**Firebox** The firebox of a stove is where the actual burning takes place. You can improve efficiency and reduce particulate emissions by controlling the temperature and air supply to the firebox.

**Firebricks** Wood burns best in a really hot firebox and so many modern stoves have highly insulating bricks lining the firebox. These reflect the heat of the flames back to the fire so that a high running temperature is reached quickly and then maintained. Firebricks can be a solid cast material, similar to fired clay, or softer vermiculite, which comes in sheets and can be cut with a suitable saw.

Grate A grate is found at the base of the firebox and is usually made from cast iron and sometimes ceramic material. The grate is either one piece of cast-iron with multiple slits or holes in it to let air through, or a series of cast iron bars arranged side by side at the base of the firebox with a gap between each. The gaps or slots are relatively narrow and only something small, like ash, falls through them. Sometimes the stove will have a riddling mechanism of some sort. Riddling is agitating the grate to make the ash fall through and make sure that air can get through to the fire. When burning coal this is very important as it needs air from below to burn well and the grate will overheat if ash is allowed to build up on it. With wood this is much less important.

Riddling usually works either by moving or shaking the whole grate in some way, by raising alternate grate bars or by a sliding movement of alternate grate bars past each other. There will be a handle on the stove to let you riddle the grate and this is best done with a little vigour and speed. Although wood burns best with an air supply from above, a grate is a way of providing an air supply from below the fire for when you are first lighting the stove or when you are refueling. Opening up the primary air vent can give that necessary boost of extra air needed to get the stove going well. In a multi-fuel stove, one that can burn both wood and coal although not together, the grate also serves as a bed for coal to burn on. Coal likes a supply of air from below, through the grate, and so a grate is more important for a coal stove than a wood burning stove.

Many wood burning stoves have no grate at all. This gains valuable space in the firebox because as well as the grate there is usually an ash pan under the grate which takes up room which could otherwise be part of the firebox. This is really important for wood burning because, compared with coal, it takes a larger volume of logs to produce the same amount of heat.

Many wood burning stoves that do have a grate do not have a riddling mechanism and here you have to do something as simple as poking at the ash a little with the tool provided with the stove. Wood burns well on a bed of ash as the ash forms an insulating layer which bounces the heat back up into the fire.

**Primary air** Primary air is the air fed in to the bottom of the firebox. This is either fed up through a grate of some sort, or just supplied through air inlets near the bottom of the firebox, sometimes in the bottom of the door.

**Secondary or tertiary air** Secondary air refers to air supplied nearer the top of the firebox. Often this air is run through channels in the body of the stove to preheat it so that when it arrives in the firebox it is hot and does not cool the fire down. One of the tricks to make wood combust efficiently is to keep the firebox temperature high. The fire we see is a chemical reaction, the oxidation of compounds in the wood, which releases heat and light. Long chemical chains in the wood that built up over many years using energy from the sun are quickly broken down into smaller parts releasing all that energy again, but in a more concentrated form. The flames we see when wood burns are in fact mainly the result of burning or oxidising impurities in the wood and the secondary air adds more oxygen to the process, giving more complete combustion.

Balancing the primary and secondary air supplies to the firebox helps to achieve high combustion temperatures, low particulate emissions and optimum efficiency.

Some stoves have a tertiary air supply. Often this is routed through channels in the stove to preheat it and is then supplied through a series of holes at the back of the firebox, either holes in the firebricks or via a horizontal metal strip with holes in built in at the base of the baffle plate. When the stove is up to temperature you can see the effect of this air supply as each air hole appears to have a jet of fire coming out of it. In fact this jet is the gases from the wood burning when they come into contact with a fresh source of oxygen.

Modern wood burning stoves can burn wood slowly a lot better than earlier models as a result of improved firebox design and cleverly managed air supplies to the gases. While you cannot completely turn down the stove you can usually reduce the air supply so it ticks over quite comfortably at lower outputs. This allows you to get some really amazing flame patterns; glowing logs at the base of the firebox and dancing flames hovering above, flickering in an out of existence as the gases catch and burn.

## Types of Stove

### Steel versus cast iron

Stoves were traditionally made of cast iron, a material that allowed stoves to be made in large numbers comparatively cheaply. Today steel fabrication techniques have made it possible to mass produce stoves using modern steels. A steel stove that is constructed using thin steel will distort; a cast-iron stove that is made using thin cast iron will crack. So it is not the type of material that decides the strength and longevity of a stove, it is its thickness and how well the body is protected from extremes of heat. Some steel stoves have a cast-iron door as a flat steel door can distort if overheated.

Cast-iron tends to retain heat for longer than steel and, correspondingly, gives out its heat over a longer period. Conversely cast iron takes longer to warm up so a steel stove can give out heat more quickly from lighting. How much heat is given out by a stove and for how long is obviously dependent on the amount of wood you feed it with and, to some extent, on the weight or mass of the metal in the stove.

### Freestanding stoves

As the name implies, freestanding stoves stand separately and away from a fireplace or any other enclosure. Heated air can freely circulate around them so care must be taken to ensure they are positioned at an appropriate distance from any materials that could be damaged by heat, including the surface underneath them.

Freestanding stoves are available in a variety of shapes and sizes with the boxed or rectangular shape being the most popular in the UK for many years. More recently the design influence of Scandinavian manufacturers has seen the introduction of round and oval shaped stoves and stoves mounted on plinths or pedestals.

The overall dimensions of stoves vary significantly and often in

relation to their nominal heat output. Stoves with larger fireboxes can be loaded with large logs and, in some models, allow the logs to be positioned front to back rather than the usual side to side. Smaller stoves can sometimes be installed within an existing fireplace opening relatively easily.

## Convection stoves

To further increase the convection element of a stove's heat output, some stoves have a second box around the body of the stove with an air gap between and ventilation holes at the top and bottom. Air enters at the bottom, is warmed by the case of the firebox, loses density, rises, and comes out of holes at the top of the stove warmer than when it went in at the bottom.

Because of this extra 'skin', the sides of convection stoves are generally cooler than other stove types, which may be an advantage if you're worried about others, especially children, touching the sides of the stove. Some range cooker stoves (see page 34) have convection sides, which allow you to build them right into your kitchen units.

## Insert and cassette stoves

Insert and cassette stoves, designed to be installed within a wall aperture, are becoming increasingly popular in the UK and offer a 'fire in the wall' effect. Cassette stoves, first invented (or at least named) by the French stove manufacturer Fondis, have two boxes (like a convecting stove) around the fire with air vents top and bottom to let the heated air into the room and some models even have a built-in fan to increase the flow of warm air into the room. They take up less space than a freestanding stove and provide a wealth of opportunity for the overall look of the installation. An insert or cassette stove installed in a plain wall offers a fairly minimal look and, if enhanced by an adjacent log store and a projecting hearth, can result in an impressive

◄ **TOP** The Dru 64cb is a good example of a cast-iron stove. This stove will hold its heat for a long time and weighs in at 180kg.

◄ **BOTTOM** The Morso 08 is a high quality minimalist take on the traditional stove and is made from steel.

▲ This La Nordica Cystal insert stove has an integral fan to blow heat into the room and is Defra exempt for smoke control areas.

installation. Surrounding an insert or cassette fire with a fire surround and mantelpiece offers a traditional look with all the aesthetic benefits of an open fire but much improved efficiency.

Insert and cassette stove models are available purpose designed to be built into an existing fireplace opening, a hole in a wall or a new chimney breast. You can build the stove into a masonry wall or into a wall made from steel studding and fireboard.

Some cassette stoves have two boxes (like a convecting stove) around the fire with air vents top and bottom to let the heated air into the room, and some models even have a built-in fan to increase the flow of warm air into the room.

Although the installation requirements vary from model to model, it is sometimes a requirement to backfill any free space behind a cassette stove with suitable insulating material. Some models of cassette

▲ The Fondis Ulys 900 is a double sided insert stove, ideal for the larger house. Heat from this stove can be ducted from the top to other rooms if needed.

stove are designed to simply slot into a standard fireplace opening.

Insert stoves do not generally have the second skin of a cassette stove so optimum heat recovery may require the insert to be installed in a bigger chamber, which itself is ventilated to the room at the top and bottom. This effectively creates a similar arrangement to a cassette stove but with purpose made vents to the chamber that can be positioned to suit your overall design. It may be a good idea to make high level vents larger than those at the bottom to account for the expansion of the heated air.

Some insert and cassette stoves are fitted with ready-made inlet and outlet spigots so that warmed air can be ducted to the same or another room. Some models have fan distribution systems available, which will blow the warmed air via ductwork throughout your home.

### Silicon carbide heaters (Slow heat release appliances)

Silicon carbide has been used as a mineral that has a high affinity to reflect heat back into the combustion chamber (burning at some 1000° C). It has a higher affinity to absorb heat than masonry. It extracts heat from contra flow flueways built within the cast, modular, component blocks and releases that heat slowly over a 12 hour period to gently warm the whole house but can be constantly fired as a conventional woodstove if preferred. Silicon carbide is a far reduced mass than that of a masonry heater, yet still doing the same job in a more conventionally sized appliance.

See page 122 for further details.

### Masonry and Kachelofen heaters

For centuries, homes of Europe (and in the last century, North America) have been heated by mass masonry heaters or Kachelofen's. The principle of such a style of heating is a small fire burned extremely hot in order to burn efficiently but distribute heat via flue channels built within the appliance and into the whole masonry mass, evenly. The uptake of heat is typically between 85-90% with the mass of material storing heat to give it up slowly to the surrounding room air envelope for many hours later. Gentle even heat permeates the whole house if doors are left open throughout the home.

Typically the masonry heater is built *insitu*, taking five days to build if professionals are employed and weighing in at 1– 4 tonnes.

See page 122 for further details.

### Box stoves

A box stove is not a technical term and if you ask a retailer for a 'box stove' they might not understand what you wanted to start with, but there is not a better word for describing this type of stove as they are square or box shaped in one form or another. Box stoves are the tra-

▶ **TOP** The Firebelly FB2 is a contemporary version of the traditional UK box stove. Made in the UK this stove will burn wood efficiently.

▶ **BOTTOM** A Stratford Ecoboiler, a multifuel stove, providing heating and hot water.

ditional shape preferred in the UK. With bigger wood burning stoves this shape can make real sense as it gives you a wide, high capacity firebox that you can load with logs. A box shaped small stove can also be installed to an existing fireplace opening with relative ease.

There is a wide range of box stoves available and of course they vary in quality and price. Box stove design is improving all the time and efficiencies in the high 70's and into the 80's are now fairly common. If you are installing your stove to an existing chimney which you do not plan to line and insulate, then choosing a less efficient, less heavily baffled model can make sense as you will probably find it more reliable on the poorly insulated chimney.

### Boiler stoves

Many stoves are available with a boiler either as a purpose built element of the stove or as an additional or add-on feature. Essentially a metal box filled with water, the 'boiler' is connected to your heating and hot water system and can provide both domestic hot water and space heating.

### Clip in boilers

Smaller 'clip-in' boilers are available for some models which can be retrofitted and usually take the place of the rear firebrick. These clip in boilers do not have a huge heat output to water, usually it is enough for your domestic hot water (hot water for washing and bathing that is) and perhaps a radiator or two.

### Wrapround boilers

A wraparound boiler is much larger and, as the name suggests, it wraps right around the firebox of the stove. These come factory fitted and so cannot be retrofitted and give higher heat outputs to water.

### Pellet stoves

▶   The Klover Smart 120 is a highly automated wood pellet cooker with an integral hopper. Designed to be installed in the house this pellet boiler can run the heating and hot water for the whole house.

Pellet stoves are becoming increasingly popular and, in some respects, are possibly more akin to modern gas boilers than traditional stoves. The wood pellets they burn are either made from pulverised wood or sawdust waste from industries that build with wood. The sawdust or pulverised wood is forced through a press at high pressure producing small, short, sausage shaped pellets, usually 6mm or 8mm in diameter. The surface of the pellet is often a little shiny due in part to the lignin in the wood, which melts at the high temperature and pressure used to create the pellets and is what binds the pellets together. Among other uses lignin is the natural water proofing agent found in the xylem, the tube system running through trees that circulates water from its roots to its leaves.

The production of wood pellets requires more energy than producing the equivalent weight of wood logs but, on a like for like basis, compares favourably with fossil fuels and non-renewable electricity. Wood pellets have low moisture content, typically around 8%, contain more energy per unit weight than wood logs, and can be easily moved around by an auger (a spinning screw in a tube) because of their uniform size. This makes pellets more akin to a traditional fuel in that the supply of pellets to the firebox can be tightly controlled. The pellets are burnt fiercely and hard in a crucible, often made from cast iron, and most pellet stoves have an ignition plug ro allow automatic lighting of the stove. Air is supplied in via a blower and the feed and burn rates controlled by a microprocessor.

The pellets are either stored in an integral hopper, which you load manually, or can be kept in a separate silo or hopper and fed to the pellet stove via an auger  or vacuum tube feed system. Pellet stoves are also available as boiler models which can provide your hot water and space heating. Some pellet stoves have a window to view the firebox and can be installed inside your home, others are installed in an outbuilding or garage.

The flames from a pellet stove are unlike those from a wood stove. Because the pellets are burnt rapidly in small quantities and in a tight-

▶   This is a DeManincor wood burning range cooker stove with matching gas hob and electric oven.

▲　The wood burning Esse Ironheart is the traditional UK range cooker stove brought up to date.

ly confined area, the flames produced form a compact wedge shape above the crucible and remain fairly constant. The dealer should have a demonstration pellet stove so that you can see and hear one in operation.

In urban areas where storage space is often at a premium, pellet stoves can make more sense than log stoves. Unlike most conventional wood stoves, they are automatic and may suit someone who does not want to manage their own wood supply or remember to light and load the stove. Pellet stoves have been in widespread use in Europe for many years.

Pellet stoves are more complex than conventional wood stoves so it's important that whoever supplies and installs your pellet stove is suitably experienced and qualified to not only fit and commission your installation but also provide the necessary regular maintenance.

### Range cooker stoves

Range cookers are traditional in the UK and, although originally designed to burn coal, revised and modified designs are now available for a wide range of fuels including wood logs. Primarily designed as cooking appliances, range cookers are equally well recognised as heating appliances, often featuring as the only source of heat in larger kitchens. Some of the models manufactured in Europe were designed from the onset to burn wood logs and provide consistent and predictable oven temperatures because the heat from the fire box circulates around the oven instead of the two sides of some traditional designs.

Range cooker stoves with integrated boilers combine cooking, heating and hot water services in a single appliance with some earlier cast-iron models, which take longer to heat up and give even oven temperatures, designed to operate all day. Some modern wood burning ranges are of lighter construction, heat up relatively quickly and can be used intermittently.

## Heat transfer and storage

### Transferring heat

Heat is transferred from its source by one of three different methods – radiation, convection or conduction. The heat from the sun is radiant heat and, as it reaches the earth, heats up the people, the ground and the objects on it. Likewise the visible flames of a wood burning fire produce radiant heat that, just like the sun, we feel as a warming of our skin. Too close and this radiant heat will burn us in much the same way that too much time in the sun can damage our skin. Much of the radiant heat from the flaming wood in a stove is contained inside a metal structure so most of it cannot reach us directly, but instead heats up the materials surrounding it.

The heated case of the stove then heats up the air surrounding the stove and it is mostly this heated air which then warms up the house. This is called convection – as the air around the stove is heated it changes its density causing it to circulate (or convect) around the room.

The third method of heat transfer is called conduction and is where heat moves from one object to another because one is cooler than the other or vice versa. Although NEVER to be recommended, putting your hand on the outside of a stove will conduct heat from the metal straight to your skin and will heat it up much more quickly than if you held your hand a few inches away.

Most stoves heat a room and its occupants by a mixture of convection and radiation, the latter coming mostly from the viewing glass.

## Storing heat

Although it is perfectly feasible to heat your entire home and meet all your hot water requirements using a single wood burning appliance, in the UK the vast majority of domestic wood burning stoves are installed as a supplementary heat source in a particular room or area. The majority are used intermittently for only a few hours a day, are generally not needed at night and, with few exceptions, cannot store heat for use later.

If you want to store heat so your stove can provide heat over an extended period or even all day, one option is to divert some of the heat generated by a boiler stove to what is called a thermal store. Essentially this is a large capacity well insulated water cylinder that can be interlinked with your boiler stove, your central heating system and even to solar panels and heat pumps.

A wood burning boiler stove is the perfect partner for a solar heating system. Solar tubes or panels can provide domestic hot water when your stove is not alight during the summer months and can supplement the domestic hot water output of the stove in the cooler months when the sunlight is not at its strongest.

Connecting your heating and hot water system lets you easily integrate multiple heat sources, solar thermal input in the warmer months from tubes or panels, and store up heat for use later on when the stove is not lit or when the sun is not out. It also allows you to burn your boiler stove a bit faster, and thus at a higher efficiency, and then use that heat later.

Water expands as it is heated so any heating system that uses water must have some capacity to deal with this expansion. There are

▲ The Aquatherm F34 provides heating and hot water for larger houses and is well suited for use with a thermal store.

two systems commonly in use, pressurised and open vented systems.

### Pressurised systems

Most new central heating systems being installed today are pressurised systems. If your central heating boiler has a little pressure gauge on the front then you almost certainly have a pressurised heating system. In a pressurised system, the expansion of the water is accommodated in an expansion vessel, which is often inside the case of the boiler or immediately alongside it. An expansion vessel is rather like a metal tank with an inflated balloon inside it. As water in the system heats up and expands flow into the tank and compresses the balloon inside creating enough space to cope with the increased volume. When the system goes off and the water cools down, the reverse happens and the balloon expands to fill the tank.

### Open vented systems

An open vented system, still very common in the UK, accommodates the expansion of the water as it is heated in an open topped tank usually located well above the boiler and often in the loft. This so-called feed and expansion tank serves no other purpose than to deal with the expansion (and contraction) of the water. It is fitted with a ball valve to replace any water lost through evaporation and an overflow usually visible on the outside of your home.

When the system is cold the level of water in the tank will be at its lowest and when the system is up to temperature it will be at its highest. Although this level varies, it is only by a few millimetres so the pressure in the system stays pretty much the same. This feed and expansion tank is open to the atmosphere, which gives the open vented system its name.

A vent pipe rises continuously from your boiler, runs up above the tank and then bends down and through a hole in the lid so that the open end finishes just above the highest water level in the tank. This is the vent pipe and allows steam to escape safely if the system were to overheat. The feed and expansion tank and its associated fittings must be rated for potentially high temperatures (a standard plastic expansion tank is not suitable) and care should be taken to stand it on a suitable base that will not degrade in the event of a leak.

The feed and expansion tank is open to the atmosphere and has a vent pipe , this gives the open vented system its name.

## Choosing the right stove

If one of the reasons you are interested in a wood burning stove is that it is a renewable form of heating and you want to make your life more sustainable then it makes sense to look first at how you can reduce your overall use of energy.

▶  The Woodfire 12i boiler stove is well suited for use in a well insulated, airtight passive house. The 12i has the ability to connect an external air-duct to provide 100% of the combustion air and at the same time has a low heat output to the room, with most of the heat going to heat water.

Insulating your house will reduce the heat you need, so you will use less fuel and save money. Insulating the walls and roof space is generally inexpensive and cost effective. Replacing single glazed windows with double or triple glazed windows will further reduce energy consumption but may be relatively expensive. Even if you cannot afford to replace all your windows, some secondary glazing and heavier curtains will help. Draught proofing is relatively cheap, simple and effective and don't forget to enquire about government approved home improvement grants designed to reduce energy consumption.

If you are designing your own home or have more ambitious energy saving plans, you might think about making your house a super insulated passive house (or PassivHaus). The basic concept is to heavily insulate the house, eliminate adventitious ventilation and recirculate the air within the home. South facing glazing lets sunshine do much of the heating in the home, which then requires the minimum amount of additional energy to maintain a comfortable temperature.

A home with a high thermal mass will absorb heat and release it slowly back into the dwelling and maintain fairly even temperatures throughout. If you are interested in learning more about this approach to house design and refurbishment then a good starting point is *The Green Building Magazine*. The magazine ties in with and comments on the activity of the The Green Building Forum where members comment and discuss all aspects of green building. For further information visit **www.greenbuildingforum.co.uk**.

## Sizing your stove

Stoves are rated according to their nominal output which is usually measured in kilowatts (kW). As a rule of thumb and for a house with average insulation, you can size the stove based on the volume of the room you wish to heat by allowing 1kW for every 14 cubic metres of volume.

Measure and multiply the length, width and height of the room in metres and then divide this figure by 14. As an example, if your sitting room is 5.5 metres long, 4 metres wide and has a ceiling height of 2 metres, this will need a stove with an output of around 3kW. If you have rooms or an open staircase directly connecting to the one where the stove will be, which you also wish to heat, add the volumes of these areas into your calculation to size a stove to comfortably heat them all. But please remember, this is a rule of thumb and you may find it useful to talk to a qualified heating engineer who can do a full heat loss calculation for you.

Do not be tempted to undersize the stove. You want to be able to heat the room properly on a cold night; and, if it is too small, you may end up burning the stove flat out in an effort to provide enough heat. Choosing a stove that has an output up to a third more than the rule of thumb calculations require gives you greater flexibility to burn it at a slower rate or for fewer hours.

## The rated heat output of a stove

It is important to recognise that the heat output claimed for a stove may have been arrived at in one of several ways. Generally, when a manufacturer has designed and built a new stove model, it will be tested in its own facilities to determine the output and overall efficiency, and the manufacturer may then choose to publish this, its own test results, in any literature for the stove.

Many manufacturers then choose to have their stoves tested by an 'approved' body such as the Heating Equipment Testing and Approval Scheme (HETAS) for conformity with published standards. HETAS is recognised by Government and publishes a comprehensive list of all the products it has tested.

This independent testing involves firing the stove with a known quantity of wood, refueling the stove at set and regular intervals, and then determining the output and efficiency over the test cycle. The test house takes full and proper account of any claims being made by the manufacturer but produces its results independently of the manufacturer and without bias.

European legislation will soon require all stoves to be tested in this way and will make it a requirement in law that any stove installed in the UK meets minimum efficiency and emission requirements.

## Heat load calculation

Your supplier should be able to perform a more accurate heat load calculation for your room and/or house based on its size and the insulation values of the walls, floor, roof and windows. This is especially important when a heating and hot water system is being designed to be run by a boiler stove. You need to be sure that the stove is up to the job, but not too big, as otherwise you will end up running it for long periods at a low output, which is inefficient. Obviously the way in which you will use your stove also has a bearing. If you light the stove when you come home from work, and burn it until you go to bed, then that is very different from lighting the stove in the morning and keeping it burning all day.

## Planning your heating system

Most often a non-boiler stove is installed and provides heat to the room it is in and perhaps adjacent rooms. The existing central heating system then provides heat and hot water throughout to rest of the house. Whilst not as common as simply installing a 'normal' stove into a living room it is possible for the entire heating system to be run by just a boiler stove. Or you may run a boiler stove in conjunction with an existing gas or oil boiler, providing all or just some of the heating and hot water needed by the house. It is a good idea to make sure that there is a radiator in the same room as the stove as this can ensure that this room heats up quickly. Wood stoves can work well in combination with many types of central heating system including radiators, under floor heating solar thermal heating and heat pumps too.

Most rooms in your house are used in different ways. For example you may want your reception rooms and bathroom to be warm most of the time that you are home, whilst your bedrooms can often be cooler. The kitchen and utility room will have other heat generating appliances like a cooker, washing machine or tumbler dryer and will need much less heat on a cold day than say your lounge. So being able to divide your house into zones which can all be heated to different temperatures and at different times will help you optimize the amount of energy you use and offer the most economy.

The design of any heating system, with or without a wood stove, is a specialised business and we would always recommend that you talk to a qualified heating engineer and particular one with experience in integrated systems.

Wood stoves can easily be part of a wholly integrated heating and hot water system and can work well in combination with many types of central heating system including under floor and solar heating.

The design of any heating system, with or without a wood stove, is a specialised business and we recommend that you always talk to a qualified heating engineer particularly one with experience in integrated systems.

Most rooms in your house are used in different ways. For example you may want your reception rooms and bathroom to be warm most of the time that you are home, while your bedrooms can often be cooler. The kitchen and utility room will have other heat generating appliances like a cooker, washing machine or tumbler dryer and will need much less heat on a cold day than say your lounge. So being able to divide your house into zones which can all be heated to different temperatures and at different times will help you optimise the amount of energy you use and offer the most economy.

## How much will it cost?

### Buying a stove

In Chapter Four there is a directory of well known stoves available in the UK with details for each model of output and efficiency. The stove market is highly competitive and prices vary widely but, as with so many things in life, you get what you pay for.

Most manufacturers will be able to give you the names and addresses of retailers in your area and a visit to one or more of them will be worthwhile. Retailers can recommend someone they know who can install your new stove.

An experienced retailer will promote the manufacturers they know provide products that are well supported with technical information and after sales service.

When choosing your stove it is worth having a look for user reviews on **www.whatstove.co.uk**. Ask the people you know who have a stove about what they think of it and what their experience was with the supplier. Whether you choose to get your stove through a bricks and mortar shop or online, there are good and bad suppliers so look for a company that can lead you through the whole process and with staff members that really know their stuff.

You can spend anywhere between £350 and £2000 on a new stove and £50 to £500 for a second hand one. Boiler stoves are more expensive and range cooker stoves can cost as much as £7000 depending on the make.

Secondhand stoves are available but deserve thorough inspection before purchase. If you elect to buy secondhand, choosing a well known make will at least offer you the opportunity to source genuine replacement parts and guidance on installation and servicing from the manufacturer.

## Installing a stove

Although no two wood stove installations are the same, all installations must comply with legal, planning and local authority requirements, which we will consider more closely in Chapter Two. Installing a stove is a specialist business and whilst you may self-install, the regulations and safety considerations apply in just the same way to DIY installations as they do to those carried out by professionals.

Whether you choose to use a professional to supply and install your stove or do it yourself, the cost of installing your new stove will, broadly speaking, fall into three areas:
- the preparation of the area where the stove will be located
- the stove, a stove pipe and, if required, a register plate
- the chimney and flueing arrangements for the stove.

led The type and age of your property will have a bearing on all three of these cost elements so the following guidance may help.

Study the manufacturer's literature to determine if there are limitations on where the stove can be installed. How close can it be to adjacent surfaces that might be damaged by heat? Is the floor beneath the stove made of suitable material or does it need further protection?

A stove pipe connects from the top of your stove to the flue or chimney that is going to take the products of combustion away to the atmosphere. Stove pipes can be purchased that match the colour and texture of your stove and are usually readily available from the stove manufacturer or a local retailer. Where your stove is installed inside a fireplace or opening, the register plate forms the transition between the stove pipe and flue or chimney and usually fits out of sight above the stove.

The design, size and integrity of the chimney or flue to which your stove must be connected, is one of the most important factors in determining how well the stove will work and how efficiently it will perform. The other factor is how dry your wood is, which is covered later on page 75. Many stove manufacturers recommend that, irrespective of age, an existing chimney should be lined and insulated to ensure optimum performance of the stove, although there are many examples, particularly in brand new properties, where a chimney lining is not required if it has been bult using suitable materials.

If you do not need any work done to your existing chimney, it will cost upwards of £200 to supply and install a stove pipe, a register plate (if needed) and a suitable cowl on the chimney. Lining an existing chimney is unlikely to cost less than £500, with the price varying with the complexity of the work. If scaffolding is required this will further increase the cost.

If your choice is to have the stove supplied and installed professionally, ask around among friends and neighbours who have had similar work done and get their recommendations on whom to use. Always get a couple of quotes and don't be afraid to ask about anything in the quotations you don't understand. And remember to plan well ahead as good installers are usually busy.

Not surprisingly, perhaps, most installers are at their busiest in the autumn and winter months so planning and executing your installation during the summer months will ensure the products you want are readily available and your installation is completed well in time

**Dupré Micalite** boards are the perfect solution when fire resistance, insulation and thermal stability are essential.

Boards are typically used to line wood burning stoves and domestic ovens where high temperature insulation is required.

Our standard densities are DMS 600 with a bulk density of 600 - 650 kg/m³ and DMS 750 at 700 - 900kg/m³, both offering the highest quality and durability in their respective categories.

Photograph cour
of Fireplace KFT

HIGH TEMP INSULATION

STRONG & DURABLE

FIRE RESISTANT

## THE LEADING NAME IN VERMICULITE FORMULATION

**Micalite** Vermiculite boards can be cut and shaped to create brick pattern effects and other bespoke decorative designs.

Micalite boards are available in a number of standard sizes and thicknesses and typical applications include:

- Linings for wood burning stoves
- Furnace and kiln linings
- Heat shields for industrial ovens

www.dupreminerals.com

We are a family run business with over 35 years experience of providing and installing wood burning stoves.

We can help you find the right stove, give expert advice, design the chimney and arrange a local installer.

Whether it be pellet stoves or log gasification boilers, thermal stores or double skin flue systems, we can advise you on every aspect of heating with wood.

**0845 226 5754**
info@stovesonline.co.uk

# Chapter Two

## Installation

◀ A Charnwood Country 4.

# Regulations

There are various local and national regulations which apply when installing a stove. They relate mainly to the chimney and connections to the chimney. Here is an overview of some of the regulations you should consider when it comes to installing your stove and chimney.

## The legal requirements

### Smoke control areas

First off you should check if you live in a smoke control area. You can do this at **www.smokecontrol.defra.gov.uk**. If you do live in a smoke control area then you should choose a Defra exempt stove. For a full list of Defra exempt stoves just click 'Exempt appliances' in the website's menu. A Defra exempt stove will burn wood while keeping below a maximum level of particulate emissions – this is to maintain air quality in densely populated places.

### Local authority

Some local authorities may inspect certain types and heights of chimneys so it is worth checking with them if they have any special requirements before you start work.

If you live in an area of outstanding natural beauty, a conservation area, or have a listed building then there may also be restrictions as to the type of chimney you can use – so contact your local authority and/or your conservation officer as appropriate. Sometimes a brick or brick effect chimney stack must be used, or sometimes an external metal twin wall flue pipe must be painted matt black. Many twin wall flues can be supplied in a matt black powder-coated finish.

### Building Regulations Document J

Stove and chimney installations come under your local authority building control must be notified of the work. There are various building regulations to consider but it is mainly Document J which deals specifically with stoves and chimneys. You can easily download this document for free from the internet at **www. planningportal.gov.uk/buildingregulations/approveddocuments/ partj/approved**. Most of the document deals with the chimney and flue pipe. It starts with a few basic requirements and then details some recommended ways of meeting them. Although the recommended ways of meeting the requirements are just that – recommendations – it is usually most practical to treat the recommendations as if they are requirements.

## Installation, 'either or'

In most local authorities (it is worth checking) in England and Wales you must either use a registered competent person stove installer, or you must perform the installation under building regulations with inspections by a building control officer. However for boiler stoves (under 40kW) you have to use a registered Competent Person wet system stove installer.

## Installing under building control

In most local authority areas you can install under building control, which means that you, your builder, or your installer can do the work. You will need a Building Regulations application form on which you will need to provide a brief description of what you propose to do and what materials you are going to use. When the job is finished it is then inspected and signed off by a building control officer. It is worth checking what charge is made for this before you start.

You need to ensure that the stove and flue are installed in accordance with Document J and the manufacturer's installation guide.

Note it is your responsibility to see that the job is certified - and if in doubt it is recommended that you appoint a professional installer.

## Competent person stove installers

There are several Competent Person schemes out there for the installation of stoves. HETAS **www.hetas.co.uk**, is the organisation most focused on stoves and has the greatest UK coverage.

There is also: the Association of Plumbing and Heating Contractors (APHC) **www.aphc.co.uk**, and the National Association for Professional Inspectors and Testers (NAPIT) **www. napit.org.uk**. Of these schemes HETAS has the greater coverage across the UK. For larger projects and contractors there is also Building Engineering Services Competence Assessement Ltd (BESCA) **www.besca.org.uk** and the National Inspection Council for Electrical Installation Contracting (NICEIC) **www.niceic.com**. You need to check that the installer is registered (they will have a current membership number) and experienced.

In the UK the course for installing a stove is usually two days. Compare this to Denmark where even chimney sweep training takes up to four years! The moral here is to make sure that the stove installer you use, whether a competent person or not, is experienced and knows what they are doing.

## Grants

There are few grants available for log burning stoves but there is a reduced rate of 5% VAT scheme for installing woodburning boiler stoves.

If the stove is a boiler stove and can only burn wood, and it is supplied and fitted by the same company, then the stove, flue and chimney products, other materials necessary for the job, and the labour associated with installing the stove are chargeable at 5%VAT.

This is a simple and easy to implement scheme, which makes choosing a woodburning boiler stove over a multifuel boiler stove a lot more attractive.

## The Renewable Heat Incentive (RHI)

This applies to the installation of Microgeneration Certification Scheme (MCS) certified pellet boilers, log boilers and woodchip boilers. There is currently a one-off payment of £2000 available called the RHI Premium Payment voucher. In Spring 2014 domestic installations can benefit from a generous payment of over 12p per kWh generated. Commercial systems can already get a payment per kWh generated, currently set at over 8p. You can read more on the Energy Saving Trust website **www.energysavingtrust.org.uk**

## Sustainability

Many people choose to install a woodburning stove to make the way in which they provide their heating more sustainable. When it comes to sustainability the phrase 'reduce and then replace' is useful to remember. The first priority should be to reduce the overall heat consumption of the house by adding insulation to the roof and walls, installing double glazing, draughtproofing, even thicker curtains – every little helps. The government's Green Deal scheme is available to provide finance for energy saving improvements in your home. Again the Energy Saving Trust **www.energysavingtrust.org.uk** is a good place to learn more about this.

Once you have improved the performance of your house you can then calculate your heat load which will let your supplier calculate the right size of stove for your house. Then you can replace at least some of your existing form of heating by using a stove burning sustainably sourced firewood.

## Stove and chimney installation

When there are problems with a stove installation the temptation is instantly to blame the stove, but the vast majority of problems have nothing to do with the stove at all, but are due to three key factors: chimney, ventilation, or fuel. Classic symptoms such as smoke coming into the room, a very sluggish fire, blackening of the window, no heat given out un-controllability and all suggest that one or a combination of these three key factors are in some way lacking. So it is very important to get these three key factors right to start with. (For some symptoms and solutions see 'Troubleshooting' on page 77). Fuel will be covered in Chapter Three so first we will take a look at the chimney and then ventilation. Afterwards we will look at some of the other things which need to be considered when installing a stove in your house, and how to get the best from your stove. We will also cover basic maintenance and troubleshoot a few common problems.

## Chimneys and flue pipe – theory and function

The chimney not only takes the flue gases, the smoke and hot gases produced by the stove; when the stove is going properly there should not actually be any visible smoke from the fire in the stove and lets them out at a safe height outside, but is also the 'engine' that drives the stove. It provides the suck needed to draw air into the firebox to make the wood burn well. The chimney also needs to provide enough draw negative pressure produced by the chimney, or how strongly the chimney sucks so that the stove does not smoke the room out when you open the door. The temperature of the air in a house at the bottom of the chimney is usually higher than the temperature of the air at the top of the chimney. This means that the air at the bottom of the chimney is more dense than the air at the top and hence air will tend to rise up the chimney. This temperature difference is vastly increased when the stove is lit – this is one of the reasons why a chimney often works better once the stove has been lit for a while as the stove and chimney have both warmed up. The better insulated the chimney the shorter this warm up process.

Wind also increases the draw by creating an area of low pressure when it moves across the top of the chimney – otherwise known as the Venturi effect. These are some recommendations relating to height, bends and orientation of the chimney.

- **Height** – the chimney should be of sufficient height to create a good draw and to get the flue gases clear of the house and any nearby windows.
- **Termination height** – the top of the chimney needs to be higher than the roof surface and not too close to nearby, taller structures so it is well out of the wind eddies and turbulence found near roof surfaces, buildings, trees and so on.
- **Bends and orientation** – this chimney should, as far as possible, go straight up. If angled sections are necessary then these should be kept to a minimum.

A common misconception is that a chimney needs bends in it to work properly. This is probably because many traditional masonry chimney's do bend because there was a fireplace on each floor of the house and each chimney had to bend away from the centre to make room for the one above. A bend in a chimney serving an open fire will also stop rain entering the chimney from falling straight down into the room. Another major consideration is tar deposits. Wood smoke has more tar than coal smoke and if the flue gases cool down too much as they go up the chimney then the tars reach their 'dew point' (the temperature at which they solidify) and condense out of the smoke and onto the walls of the chimney. These tars can build up over time and are highly flammable. If they catch fire the resulting chimney fire can burn at extremely hot temperatures (over 1200°C) and so is potentially life threatening and can end up setting fire to the rest of the house, and will often irreparably damage the chimney. Reducing tar deposits helps reduce the risk of chimney fire and can be achieved by:

- Making sure that the chimney is insulated so that the gases do not cool too much
- Making sure that the internal diameter is not oversized, which will help the gases travel faster up the chimney
- Making sure that the internal surface of the chimney should be smooth, giving a low surface area for deposits and a low resistance to the flow of the flue gases
- Choosing a chimney with a round cross section as the flue gases move more slowly in the corners of square chimneys

In the UK all chimney and flue pipe connections tend to be with the male end downwards – an easy way to think of this is that if you poured water down from the top of the chimney it should end up in the stove – or in the tee on the back of the stove if you used the rear exit. Don't pour water down your chimney as that's a really bad idea.

These tars and deposits also reduce the internal area of the chimney so it will not work well and will need to be swept frequently. A chimney that has been designed for a modern woodburner will also need sweeping less often than a badly designed chimney – for example a simple square brick chimney in a Victorian town house.

### Modern stoves have low flue gas temperatures

A modern, efficient, woodburning stove has relatively low flue gas temperatures (e.g. below 250°C when up and running) compared with older stoves and especially compared with open fires in a fireplace, where most of the heat is wasted up the chimney. For this reason the design and insulation of a chimney for a modern woodstove is even more vital both to keep the chimney drawing well and to reduce tar deposits.

### Sweeping access

It is very important to be able to sweep the chimney with ease as a woodburning stove should be swept at least once a year, probably twice, and possibly more often. It is usually possible to sweep through stoves if the top flue exit has been used, by removing the baffle inside the stove. The resulting soot ends up back in the stove where it can be removed. If the rear exit of the stove is used then a 90° tee or 135° tee is used so that the soot ends up in the dead leg of the tee where is can be removed and where it cannot block the chimney or flue. Where a stove cannot be swept through then an access door should be designed into the chimney.

## Types of chimney and flue pipe

Now we will move on to consider various different types of chimney, products available, and a little information on how these are used, however please be aware that this is not intended as a comprehensive DIY guide to using these products. You will need to refer to building regulations and/or have the installation carried out by an experienced installer. The regulations have not been regurgitated in this book as they change over time and too many to describe here.

### Single skin flue pipe

This is often used to connect the stove to the chimney. This has the added benefit of passing a little more heat to the room as it is uninsulated, but as you will have gathered already losing, too much heat

▲    Examples of enamelled steel flue pipes on left and stainless steel flue pipes on right.

like this is not good for the functioning of the chimney so the length of flue pipe should be kept within reason. Flue pipe is often thicker than, for example, flexible stainless steel chimney liner, and so is well suited as the first part of the chimney connected to the stove, which has to withstanding the highest temperatures. Single skin flue pipe can be cut to length as needed and bends and adjustable lengths are available making it easier to connect to a fixed chimney.

The lengths are sealed using fire cement, high temperature silicone, and in some cases ceramic fire rope.

If you are running single skin flue pipe up to connect to an insulated chimney coming through the ceiling above then make sure that you move over to the insulated chimney well below the ceiling height so that the ceiling doesn't get too hot.

### Register plate

Where you are installing a stove into an existing masonry chimney, whether you are using a flexible chimney liner or not, a register plate is used to seal off the chimney so that it is only the flue pipe which goes up through it. The edges of the register plate are sealed to the chimney with mortar or fire cement so the chimney only draws air through the stove. The register plate also stops any stones or debris that may fall down the chimney from landing on top of the stove, or falling into your room or onto you. If a flexible chimney liner is used with insulating backfill like leca then the register plate also holds this, stopping it from pouring out into the room. If no liner is used then the plate should have an access panel built in to allow for chimney sweeping.

A register plate should be made of metal and can be custom made by the better suppliers and installers.

If you do not use a liner then the flue pipe should only poke up a little above the plate – say around 100mm. Many people think that it should go as high as possible – this is not the case.

### Enamelled or stainless steel

Single skin flue pipe comes as enamelled or stainless steel. Enamelled flue pipe is available in matt and gloss black and white and a range of other more specialist colours. Stainless steel flue pipe can be spray painted as required. The paint will not cure completely until the stove has been lit so be aware that before this it can be easily scratched or marked. Often the stainless steel is a better fit to twin wall and liner fittings, and can last longer than enamelled flue pipes which are made from mild steel.

The lengths are sealed using fire cement, high temperature silicone, and in some cases ceramic fire rope.

### Flexible stainless steel chimney liner

Existing brick chimneys, or chimneys made with clay or concrete liners often need to be relined and insulated in order to make them suitable for a modern wood stove. The easiest way to do this is to pull a

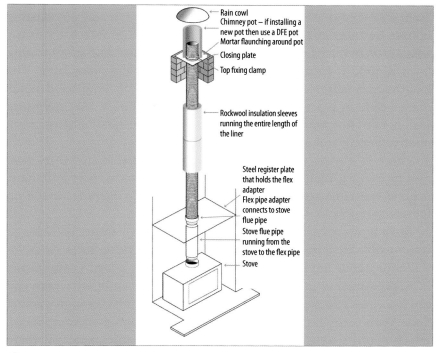

Rain cowl
Chimney pot – if installing a
new pot then use a DFE pot
Mortar flaunching around pot
Closing plate
Top fixing clamp

Rockwool insulation sleeves
running the entire length of
the liner

Steel register plate
that holds the flex
adapter
Flex pipe adapter
connects to stove
flue pipe
Stove flue pipe
running from the
stove to the flex pipe
Stove

▲ A typical flue liner installation.

continuous length of flexible stainless steel chimney liner down the chimney and surround it with insulation.

The chimney liner has a round, smooth inner surface and ensures that no smoke can leak out (which scan happen in old chimney stacks).

### In situ casting

Another way of lining an existing chimney is by using an insulating concrete-type product. A long balloon is pulled down the chimney, held off the sides so that it is central, inflated, and the bottom end sealed off. The insulating concrete-type material is then poured down around the balloon and allowed to set resulting in a smooth, insulated, masonry chimney. This can also strengthen a chimney, filling in cracks and voids in the brick or stonework. This system needs to be installed by specialist installers who have the equipment necessary.

## Twin wall insulated chimney

Twin wall chimney is used to make new chimneys, usually in existing houses but also in new builds. It can be run either internally or externally as required. An inner skin of stainless steel has an insulating layer around it (usually 25mm thick) and then the outer layer. The lengths normally twist or screw together and a locking band holds them firmly in place. Various lengths, bends, elbows, tees, floor and wall penetration components are available off-the-shelf making this a relatively easy and quick product to install.

There is a wide range of roof flashings available suited to most roof types – e.g. slate, tile, flat roofs, corrugated roofs, polycarbonate. A good specialist company can also have custom flashings made up for special roofs like sedum.

Most types of twin wall chimney only need a clearance of 50mm to combustible materials (eg floorboards), again making for a quick installation, while not taking up too much valuable space in your house.

Make sure that you choose a type of twin wall chimney where you can use closed floor penetration components to come through the first floor. With many types you still have to use a ventilated component, which could potentially spread smoke and fumes upstairs if there was a fire downstairs.

## Pumice chimney systems

Pumice is volcanic rock product and ideal for making chimneys as not only does it form a physically strong structure, it is also an inherently insulating material that can withstand the very high temperatures of a chimney fire, which most other types of chimney cannot. Pumice is a chimney system best suited to newbuild or where there are major renovations taking place. There are two main types: Pumice liners which are used inside a brick or block chimney stack with the gap filled in with an insulating backfill like leca, and modular pumice chimney systems which slot together (a bit like giant lego) to form the finished stack all in one go. Of these modular systems some are a two block system with an inner block and outer block, while there are also single block systems available.

The materials of modular systems are epensive but modular systems are fast to install and economical with space so can be more attractive than non-modular systems. Corbels suited to an externally rendered or a brick clad stack are available with a chimney pot and finishing cap at the top to finish.

Modular pumice systems are also well suited to timber frame buildings as they can be installed freestanding on their own mini foundation, with stainless steel rods fixed into the foundation and held under tension at the top of the chimney for added strength and flexibility. Non structural timbers can also be run right up against the finished chimney.

### Flexible stainless steel liner

Flexible stainless steel chimney liner comes by the metre and is either pulled down or up the chimney. This is a two man job with one feeding the liner in from the coil, the other pulling on a rope attached to the liner. The insulation comes in the form of leca insulating backfill, which is poured in to fill up the space around the liner and chimney, rockwool sleeves which are taped around the liner as it is installed, or a blanket-like materials which simple wrap and fasten around the liner. Vermiculite compresses if it gets damp leaving the top part of the liner (where the flue gases are at their coolest and hence in most need of insulation) uninsulated and so when using an insulating backfill it it generally best to opt for leca which is not compressible

### Chimney pots

A chimney pot is a familiar sight in the UK and visually finishes a masonry chimney off while also raising the height a little further away from the roof of the house and the chimney stack. Chimney pots come in many shapes and sizes – one of the most common and simple pots is the rolltop but there is a plethora of styles and colours to choose from. Have a look at any other houses nearby and see what style of pots they have.

The pot is mortared on to the top of the chimney and the cement is flaunched so that the water runs off and away. Always use waterproofer in a flaunching mix to prevent frost damage. A Decorative Fuel Effect (DFE) chimney pot serves the dual function of acting as a chimney pot and rain cowl and can be an easy and practical way of simply finishing off the chimney.

### Chimney cowl

The main function of a chimney cowl is to stop rain from getting down inside the chimney. Rain not only cools the chimney down, making it take longer for the chimney to warm up but it can also potentially damage the chimney. Rain water is slightly acidic and, when combined with some of the acid products present in varying amounts in smoke, can eat away at your chimney. There are various styles of cowl; some are suited to more extreme weather conditions – ask your supplier for a recommendation. Downdraught is when wind blows or gusts down the chimney resulting in puffs of smoke coming out of the stove. (Read more in the toubleshooting section page 80).

Anti-downdraught cowls can be used to stop or reduce downdraught and there is a wide variety available. Some are very compact and unobtrusive; there is a veddette type in an 'H' shape, and spinning cowls which will improve chimney draw if there is wind to make them spin. They all stop or reduce wind blowing directly down the chimney. Spinning cowls are good in certain instances but you need to be able to access them easily as they need regular cleaning.

### Chimney fans

In extreme cases where chimney draw is very poor and cannot be improved in any other way a chimney fan can be used to literally suck the smoke out of the chimney. These are available in a variety of sizes and types to suit most applications but should really be viewed as a last resort after other ways of improving the chimney draw have been tried.

## Stove room ventilation

The fire needs a supply of air in order to be able to burn well, and when you open the door of your stove even more air is drawn through the stove and up the chimney. This means that somehow air needs to get into the room where your stove is. For low output stoves it may be that the existing ventilation in your house, such as window trickle vents, gaps under doors and so on, is sufficient, but do bear in mind that improvements such as fitting double glazing can reduce this ventilation. It can make sense to install dedicated ventilation even if you are not required to by the regulations.

If you have extractors such as a cooker hood extractor fan in a room connected to the room with the stove in it then you need to increase the ventilation to the stove. It can also make sense to provide a source of incoming air for the extractor so that it does not fight the stove so much for air.

Room ventilators are readily available and can be fitted with a core drill making it a very simple part of the job.

In the increasingly well sealed modern house stoves which are room sealed are increasingly being used. These stoves take some or all of the air they need directly through an external air duct. This reduces draughts in the room and improves the air tightness of the house.

## Hearth

Your stove needs to sit on a non combustible hearth. If the floor is flammable then the hearth protects it from the heat given out by the stove and is also where any sparks or embers which accidentally fall from the stove should end up landing. The hearth also gives you a visible area around the stove, which should be kept clear of flammable items like carpets, chairs, etc. There are some minimum sizes laid down in Document J – essentially the minimum size of the hearth for a freestanding stove should be 840mm x 840mm, with at least 150mm to the sides of the stove and 300mm to the front. If the stove will be used with the door open sometimes then increase the distance to the front of the hearth.

Hearths are often made of stone or masonry like slate or bricks but off-the-shelf hearths made from glass, resin or stone are increasingly popular.

If the temperature under the stove has been tested and does not reach over 100°C then a thin 12mm hearth can be used, if not then the hearth has to be a lot thicker.

The hearth and floor under the hearth needs to be able to take the weight of the stove. Most stoves are not all that heavy but in some cases you may need to pay special attention to this.

### Clearances and heat shielding

Your stove and flue pipe can potentially get very hot – 300°C is not uncommon for a flue pipe, and in the very extreme case of a chimney fire this can rise to over 1000°C so it is a good idea to make sure that anything flammable around the stove and flue pipe is either far enough away or heat shielded to protect it.

Most stove manufacturers state the minimum distances which the stove should be from noncombustible and combustible materials and you need to keep to them. Single skin flue pipe has to be three times its diameter away from combustible materials, so a 150mm flue pipe needs to be at least 450mm away from something flammable. Often this is impossible as the single skin flue may have to run near a wooden lintel or mantel piece and so it needs heat shielding. Pay special attention to things like wooden lintels, curtains, skirting boards, wiring, plugs and furniture near the stove.

A good way of heat shielding is by using 12mm fireboard with a 12mm airgap behind. The air gap can be easily achieved by cutting strips of the fireboard to use as spacers. Remember not to use metal fixings near the flue pipe as these will transfer heat through to the wood. In many installations 'experienced' installers have heat shielded using thin metal fixed directly to the wood – not a very safe solution as you can imagine.

# Carbon monoxide alarms

It is a requirement under Document J, to instal a carbon monoxide (CO) alarm and worth doing anyway. CO is a byproduct of combustion and the more inefficient the combustion the more is produced. Under some circumstances it can be possible for this CO to leak into the house from the stove or flue pipe. CO is an odourless, tasteless

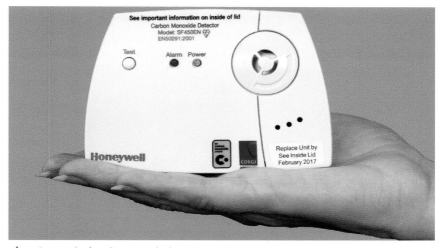

▲   An example of a carbon monoxide alarm.

gas, which has a variety of effects such as causing tiredness, headaches and flue-like symptoms and can in extreme cases make you pass out or worse. Wood smoke leaking into your house is perhaps of a little less concern than coal smoke as wood smoke tends to make you cough and therefore alert you to the problem, but you should still fit a CO alarm whether burning wood or coal.

Fitting a CO alarm will alert you to raised CO levels. Remembering to maintain your stove, flue pipe, and chimney properly, as well as running your stove in the right way (please see 'checklist for safe and efficient woodburning' on page 76) are the best ways to stop CO becoming a problem in the first place.

## Fireguards

A fireguard or nursery guard is used to stop children being able to get too close to a stove. Certainly where there are young children in the house a fireguard can give piece of mind to the parents and let them concentrate on one of the other many things they need to pay attention to. Fixtures for a fireguard should always be installed where there are children under 12 in the house.

A useful tip is that a children's playpen (the hexagonal type), folded out and fixed at the wall either side of the the stove makes a very effective, and affordable nursery guard. The door section can be placed by the fire door to let you load the stove easily.

## Wood storage and access to firewood

Storing wood near your stove is a good idea as you do not want to be bringing small loads of wood in from outside all the time, especially when it is warm inside. Aim to store at least a days wood near your stove. Depending on your stove this could be anything from half to three wheelbarrows of wood. The wood will also dry a little further while stored inside. Many people use a simple log basket but you might also consider building a woodstore into a wall or corner of a room. Inset stove installations often incorporate a woodstore either under the stove or to the side, which is practical and looks good too.

It is also worth thinking about the route you will use to bring in the wood from outside to your internal store – making it as short as possible will save you a lot of time in the long run.

## Hot water and thermal stores

A hot water tank lets you store up hot water to use for washing and bathing. Often a simple and effective system is to have the stove heat up the water tank first and only once the tank has reached a set temperature does the pump for the radiators (or other form of heating) start. It is always recommended to install a solar enabled hot water tank even if you are not intending to install solar thermal – the extra solar coil does not really add much to the price of the tank.

Solar thermal is the perfect partner for a boiler stove as the stove provides your hot water and heating when the solar input is low, and the solar panels then take over to provide hot water in the warmer months when you are not using your stove.

▶   An example of a stove (Dovre Astroline 4) which has some storage room for logs.

A thermal store is a term used for a large, well insulated, hot water tank. A thermal store lets you store up heat for use later on which means you can program your heating to come on in the morning before the stove is lit. By heating a large body of water you can also run your stove relatively fast (the most efficient and safe way of using a stove, especially a wood stove) without overheating your house, plus it means you do not have to burn your stove all day if you do not want to. A thermal store will also let you easily run your stove in conjunction with solar panels.

A remote tank thermometer is a great idea as you can visually see how hot the water in your thermal store is, which then lets you decide whether you should load up your stove or not.

### Load unit and flue thermostat

A load unit is essential for the serious boiler stove user. The load unit pumps the water around the boiler in the stove and only when the water temperature has come up to above 60° C does it allow hot water out to the heating and hot water system and cool water back in. The high temperature is always maintained by the unit, which greatly improves heat output and efficiency, and reduces tar deposits and corrosion. This also means that the water tank only receives hot water from the stove so stored hot water in the tank is maintained.

A flue thermostat is used to switch on the load unit pump by detecting when the flue pipe of the stove is hot. This stops the potential problem of the stove leaching heat from the hot water tank.

### High temperature header tank

For vented heating systems (still most common for boiler stoves in the UK) you need a high temperature header tank. This header tank is the last ditch safety device into which steam can be vented in the event of the stove overheating, which is why the tank must be boil-proof as it can potentially get very hot.

▶   A Hunter Herald 14, which has a boiler option, outputting 13kW, enough to provide hot water and run a reasonable number of radiators.

## Heat leak device

A heat leak device does pretty much what is says on the packet – it takes heat away from the system if it is getting too hot. At least one form of heat leak device should be installed, the usual preference is for there to be two. For vented systems a heat leak radiator is usually installed.

- **Vented** – at the top of the system there is a header tank which is open to the air. As the water temperature rises it expands and the level in the tank rises and visa versa.
- Most of the boiler stove installations in the UK are vented, although that is slowly changing.
- **Unvented** – the system is sealed and the water expansion is taken up into an expansion vessel as opposed to a header tank.

Most of the boiler stove installations in the EU are unvented.

A heat leak radiator is a radiator, to which hot water can flow via thermosyphoning, essential when water flows through a heating system due to the temperature difference between the hot water coming from the stove, the 'flow', and the cooler returning water, the 'return'. The hotter water is less dense and the cooler water more dense, hence the hotter water tends to rise and the cooler water tends to fall. To get this working right takes experience and can be tricky. Allow the stove to dump heat if necessary. A common practice is to use a large towel rail or large radiator in a bathroom as the heat leak radiator – the problem here is that you then have a radiator which can potentially get very hot and which you cannot control in a room that is used in your house. The ideal is to locate the heat leak radiator in an unused space and control the water gong to it with a valve and pipe thermostat so that it only comes on in the event of overheating or a power failure.

Boiler stoves installed on unvented systems have an overheat safety valve and coil fitted. If the water in the stove goes over a certain temperature mains cold water is flushed through the coil in the boiler, taking the heat, which is then discharged outside.

Installing a boiler stove is a lot more complicated than a dry stove in terms of overall system design as well as the actual installation itself and following the regulations should be done by a registered Competent Person

### Pellet stoves

Pellet stoves are more complicated to install than log burning stoves and installation should definitely be left to trained engineers or installers. A pellet stove usually requires an electricity supply which is an important consideration.

Make sure that whoever supplies and installs your pellet stove can also be booked in for regular servicing and maintenance, and that they hold stocks of the main spare parts needed.

## Using your stove

### The first time you light your stove

When you first light the stove make sure the windows in the room are open and close the door to the room and leave it empty for as much of the time as possible, although you need to attend to the fire. You should only light a small fire for a short time and then let the stove cool. The next fire can be a little hotter and last a little longer. Refer to the manufacturer's guidelines for exact guidance. This is the time when the paint, sealants, fire cement, etc on and in the stove and flue pipe cure. You can expect a strange smell and sometimes a little white smoke coming from the stove and or flue pipe. This is completely normal.

After the first few firings you can use the stove as normal and it is important that you get the stove and flue nice and hot for a good few hours to make sure that you properly cure the paint. Again you may need to open windows and close the door to the room until the paint has cured.

### Checklist for safe and efficient burning

- Only burn seasoned firewood.
- Stay with the stove while you are lighting it and up until you have loaded it and turned it down to normal running temperature. Keep monitoring the stove while it is burning.

- Light the stove using dry kindling to heat up the firebox fast. You can use paper or firelighters to burn the kindling. Place the kindling in such a way that flames and air can get to as many part of the kindling as possible. A pick-up-sticks pile is preferable to a bunched stack.
- The air vents should be fully open when first lighting the stove. You might also crack open the ash-pan door and or the door to the firebox. Refer to manufacturer's guide lines.
- When the fire is going well add some bigger logs. When these are burning, shut down the air a little. If your stov has primary and secondary air controls then shut down the primary and control the stove using the secondary air.
- Do not slow burn or slumber burn.
- Do not turn the stove down for the night.
- Wait till the logs have burnt down to a bed of glowing embers before adding more logs. Turn the air up a little to help the new logs catch fire, then back down again once they are going.
- When the stove is burning properly (other than when it is first lit or when it has just been refueled) there should be no visible smoke coming out of the chimney, just a heat haze. If there is smoke then you are probably doing something wrong.
- Sweep your chimney at least once a year before the burning season. The frequency of sweeping depends on how much you burn and what you burn.
- An indication as to how often you should sweep the chimney is given by the amount of deposits that are produced at each sweeping. Frequent wood burners should sweep at least twice a year. Consult an experienced chimney sweep if in doubt.
- With all stoves, and particularly modern high efficiency stoves, it is important to get the stove and chimney hot before you start turning it down. Turn the stove down too soon and you'll get a stove that tends to smoke, blacken's the glass and won't burn properly.

Please see page 117 for more detailed instructions on lighting your fire.

### Troubleshooting

The majority of problems to do with stoves are in fact nothing to do with the stove at all. The lion's share of problems are due to a poor chimney, poor ventilation, or poor fuel. This also holds true for pellet stoves.

Although it is possible to give yourself the best chance of success by having your chimney designed by an expert the fact is that each installation is different and even the most perfectly designed chimney may not work in all locations.

Below is detailed some information on how to work out what the possible causes might be, and possible solutions. However it is a good idea to:

- Check that the chimney is not blocked and make sure it has been swept.
- Check that the flue pipe connecting the stove to the chimney is not blocked and has been swept.
- Check that the the area between the baffle plate of the stove and the flue exit has not been blocked by debris.
- Check that the air can get into the firebox of your stove – make sure the ash pan is empty and the grate clear of ash (bear in mind that this is just to rule out potential problems – often, day-to-day you would use a woodstove with some ash in).

You can expect more problems if it is a very still day with no wind and or a very warm, low pressure day

## Maintenance

### Sweeping and cleaning

The most important thing to do is to sweep the chimney regularly, sweep the flue pipe, and clean out the inside of the stove including the baffle plate, behind the baffle plate, and the flue exit on the stove.

### Ash

In most woodstoves some ash can be allowed to build up on the grate (if the stove has a grate) as wood burns best with a supply of air from above. You should empty the ashpan (if there is one) regularly. Remember that the ash may still be hot, so use a galvanised metal bucket or special ash caddies, which can be attached to your vacuum cleaner.

## In the summer
In the summer when the stove is not in use open the door a little to keep the stove and chimney well ventilated.

## Lighting your stove for the first time in the season
Before you light the stove for the first time check that the chimney and flue are not blocked as summer is a classic time for birds (especially jackdaws) to try to nest in your chimney. It is a good idea to sweep the chimney before the start of the season.

Check the baffle for damage, look behind the baffle and the flue exit for blockages, check the grate for damage and clear the ash from the grate and ash-pan.

## Cleaning the body of the stove and covering minor scratches and marks
If the stove has marks on the surface and or dirt, when it is cold, you can wipe it with a damp cloth to clean it. If there is a minor scratch a quick spray with the right heat resistant spray paint may do the trick. If the scratch mark is a little deeper you may need to rub down the area with some wire wool first before spraying. Remember to mask off areas like the window of the stove and the surroundings and to ventilate the room well. Several light layers of paint are better than one thick layer. Do not use too much paint as if it is too thick it may peel off in the end.

Some stoves are polished with graphite stove polish although most modern stoves are finished with spray paint. If the finish on your stove is polish then you can polish it every so often to get it looking like new. The best way is to mix some stove polish with a solvent like white spirit to the consistency of single cream, apply it evenly to the stove with a paint brush, allow to dry (5–10mins at room temp), and then buff up with a large brush like a shoe brush or large bath brush.

To clean your stove glass

Most stoves these days have airwash to keep the glass clearer but however good the airwash the glass will still develop some deposits and marks over time.

If the window is very tarred then a nice hot fire to get the stove hot will tend to burn off a lot of the tar and the rest can be cleaned with a number of good cleaning products on the market.

# Troubleshooting

| Symptom | Cause | Solution |
|---|---|---|
| Stove smokes into the room in puffs | This is probably downdraught caused by wind blowing down the chimney. It may only happen under certain wind conditions. | Insulate the chimney if you have not already done so, raise the height of the chimney, fit an anti-downdraught cowl. |
| Stove continually smokes into the room | This may only happen under certain wind conditions. It may be caused by lack of ventilation. To check this open a window – does that solve the problem? Is there an extractor fan fitted in a room near the stove? This is a classic problem in pubs and restaurants. Turn it off – does that solve the problem? It may be caused by a poor chimney – does it improve once the stove has been going a while? In very rare cases this can be due to 'pressure difference' – when the air pressure in the room with the stove is lower than the pressure in another room or outside the house, which results in air being drawn the wrong way down the chimney. This will generally only happen when there is wind. | If opening the window solved the problem then you probably need to fit a vent to the room. There may be a vent already but it may be blocked. If it improves after turning an extractor off then you will need to install more ventilation to the room and possibly ventilation to the room where the extractor is fitted. Or fit a stove that can take its combustion air directly from outside. If it improves after the stove has been going a while then consider insulating your chimney if you have not done so already. You might also consider raising the chimney height a little. If the problem is pressure difference then the only real solutions are to move the stove to another side of the house and another chimney if possible (which may work) or fit a flue fan. |
| Stove is hard to light | As above | As above Also try opening the ash-pan door a little; you may also try opening the door of the stove a very little (e.g. 10–20mm). Make sure that you stay with the stove if you do this and shut the door(s) when it is going well. |

| Symptom | Cause | Solution |
|---|---|---|
| Stove gives out little heat, the window blackens up very fast<br><br>Stove burns OK flat out, but is hard to turn down. | It is likely that your wood is not well seasoned. Split a log and test the split face with a moisture meter – if it is above 25% then it is not well seasoned.<br>Look at the end grain of the log – most species of well seasoned wood have splits in the end grain of the log.<br>Smell the log – wet wood tends to have a characteristic smell which you can recognise over time.<br>Try burning some kiln dried wood or sawdust briquettes which are guaranteed to be dry – does that improve the performance?<br>You may also simply be burning the stove too slowly – you should have good visible flames, minimal smoke inside the firebox, and not visible smoke coming out of the chimney (just heat haze) when it is burning well. | Get a firewood moisture meter if you have not already got one. If your fuel is not well seasoned then you should complain to your supplier if it was sold to you as seasoned.<br>Consider sourcing your wood 1–2 years in advance and seasoning it yourself by stacking it well exposed to the wind but protected from direct rain. It should be cheaper to buy your wood unseasoned in bulk.<br>Your stove supplier should be able to estimate your yearly consumption for you.<br>Consider burning kiln dried logs or sawdustbriquettes – it is initially a more expensive option but can actually work out cheaper than burning badly seasoned wood as you will not have to burn as much to get the same amount of heat.<br>Follow the steps in the 'checklist for safe and efficient woodburning' on page 76. |
| Stove burns very fast and is hard to control | Check that the baffle is in place – if not then site it correctly or buy a new one if it has burnt out.<br>Check that you are using all the air controls on the stove correctly.<br>You may have a very strong chimney draw. | If you have very strong draw then fitting a flue damper or a draught stabiliser should help. |

New!

# The right stove for your wallet and for the environment

A stove with added cosiness! New and more efficient combustion technology make Contura i5 the stove insert that produces more heat using less wood. With Sweden's only Swan-labelled stove insert, you can be even cosier and have a clear conscience.

**Best heating economy** High efficiency produces more heat using less wood
**Most resource-efficient** The only Swedish Swan labelled insert
**Modern design** Clean lines that give style to any environment
**See the fire through the clear glass** New efficient combustion technology minimises soot build-up

Part of **NIBE**    contura.eu

*Contura*
Stoves for every home

# Chapter Three

## Wood and its source

## Wood for your stove

By now you have probably thought long and hard about the type of stove you are going to buy, its installation and any work that needs doing to your chimney. So now is the time to think about your wood fuel supply.

About 100 years ago 4% of Britain was covered by woodland. Now the figure is around 12% so, although you might think that getting firewood should be easy, the following facts may help explain why it isn't:

- The UK is one of the least wooded places in Europe. Only 12% of the UK is woodland, compared with an average of 44% for other parts of Europe and 75% for Sweden in particular.
- In the last 100 years, 46 broadleaved woodland species have become extinct in the UK.
- In 1980, native species accounted for only 5% of the trees planted in the UK. Thanks to the efforts of conservation and organisations like The Woodland Trust, this figure has risen to over 40%.

In 2007, under the auspices of The Forestry Commission, the government published 'The Woodfuel Strategy for England' focusing attention on the future of wood as a fuel. Similar papers were published for Wales and Scotland. Research in England had shown that around 4 million tonnes of the wood grown annually was never harvested so the government set a target to increasingly harvest this annual growth so that by the year 2020 an extra 2 million tonnes of wood a year will become available.

Wood is different from all other heating fuels. Gas and electricity are effectively 'piped' into your house so once you have an agreement with the supplier you simply draw as much fuel as you want. Heating oil and coal are a little more like firewood in that you store them at your home, check how much you have from time to time and

order new stocks when you are running low. However, and in common with each other, gas, electricity, oil and coal are all sourced from well-regulated companies supplying a consistent product at a price which, can very quickly be compared via the phone or internet. This is not the case with firewood.

Some argue that wood is the finest heating fuel of all. It is sustainable, often locally produced and competitive with the cost of other fuels. It may become even more so as fossil fuel prices continue to rise.

Enthusiasts suggest that when your wood store is full of seasoned wood ready to burn, concerns about Russian pipelines, road haulage disputes and the influence of OPEC are replaced with the security and comfort of having your own store of energy. Firewood is also said to offer more than just security and control. As, over time, you get to know your suppliers and maybe gather some wood yourself, links develop with the countryside and with the people who live and work there.

We once had a strong tradition of burning wood for light, cooking and heating, from the great country manors with their mighty hearths for roasting pigs to the peasants in Thomas Hardy novels scouring the Wessex heath lands for thorn twigs and gorse. This ancient wood-burning tradition was largely lost after the discovery of vast quantities of coal, gas and oil in and around the British Isles but these fossil fuel reserves are diminishing and have witnessed the renaissance of wood as a fuel.

Interestingly, the move to using more of our own firewood coincides with a strong movement towards growing more of our own food. Long derelict allotments are once again thriving under the careful stewardship of a new generation of gardeners. People have found real pleasure in the exercise of growing food and the great sense of community that usually seems to accompany it. Firewood sits very comfortably with this general desire for more control of the food and fuel that we bring into our homes. For some it offers a more sustainable and environmentally sound lifestyle, a chance to widen our network of friends and improve what is often called our 'social capital'.

Using wood as fuel may give you and your home a warm inner

glow, but you need to know at least something about the trees that provide your firewood, how to tell good logs from bad, and how to harvest or buy your firewood. Just as importantly, you need to know how to prepare and store your precious wood.

## Woodland management

Trees are living things so before looking at their management it's helpful to know what's going on in a tree and what helps trees to flourish. The study or profession of looking after single trees is called 'arboriculture' and the study or the profession of looking after groups of trees and woodlands is called 'silviculture'. Tree surgeons, woodsman and foresters are the professionals trained to look after our trees.

### Tree fundamentals

Despite their apparent simplicity, trees are surprisingly complex. Trees have four parts – the roots, the stem (or trunk), the branches and the leaves.

The roots provide the tree with a secure anchorage in the surrounding earth and supply the tree with most of the moisture and minerals that it needs to live and grow. While it is commonly believed that the roots of a tree are as large and expansive as its branches, this is mostly incorrect. Just look at any tree blown over by the wind and you will see that the roots make up a relatively small part.

The tree trunk or stem has two functions. First, it elevates the plant to give its leaves the best opportunity to collect energy from the sun, and second it acts as a store for the sugars created in the leaves and converted to starch. The branches of a tree form the intricate support network for the leaves, which themselves can take many forms from the 'big flat plates' of the sycamore tree to the 'needles' we find with conifers. The leaves and the bark covering the younger twigs of a tree contain chlorophyll, the powerhouse of virtually all plant life.

Chlorophyll is critical to the process of photosynthesis, the means by which, via the absorption of sunlight, plants can convert the carbon dioxide and water vapour in the atmosphere into carbohydrates

▲   A trunk cross section.

and sugars, the food on which the tree feeds and grows.

When looking at the cross section of a freshly cut log it is possible to see how the tree has grown and the structure of the wood. Starting from the outside there is the outer bark, which is there to protect the tree, like a skin. Depending on the species of tree and the inherent dangers in that tree's natural environment the outer bark can protect the tree from fire and physical damage in addition to providing a waterproof skin.

Between the outer bark and the inner wood is a very thin layer of living cells, the cambium, which each year grows into a new layer of wood and thickens the bark. In some species of tree these 'annual rings' are fairly obvious and the tree's age can be determined by counting them. This is easiest to do with oak, ash, elm and sweet chestnut. These dark and light annual rings are not, as some believe, winter and summer but spring and summer wood. The lighter part of the annual ring is the rapidly grown springwood and the darker part is the slower growing summer wood.

The wood itself is in two parts, the heartwood and the sapwood. The sapwood is usually light in colour and is a mass of tiny pipes through which water flows up the tree. The heartwood is dead and darker in colour as all the pipes are blocked up. The heartwood serves to strengthen the tree but a tree can survive quite easily without it as is proved by the many hollow trees that exist.

## Managing wood

The secret to woodland management is balance, a careful balance of growing trees of all ages and only harvesting the volume of wood that the woodland can spare or will easily replenish in a few years. Nowadays it is also important to balance the production of wood and timber with the needs of our wildlife and the protection of any sites of archaeological significance in the woodland. Increasingly people are attracted into woodlands so the forester must also balance this rising demand for woodland recreation with the needs of wood production and wildlife conservation.

Firewood is harvested in a number of different management operations but is generally of secondary importance to production of the good quality timber to be used in building, flooring, furniture and fencing. However, over recent years the rising demand for firewood and a desire to safeguard our woodlands through the reintroduction of more traditional management techniques has led to a rise in the use of ancient silvicultural techniques where the production of firewood may be the primary aim.

Clear felling, or 'clear-cutting' as the Americans call it, is the practice of felling all of the trees within a given area. It is the most common management system within plantation forestry, whether the trees are conifers or broadleaves. A forester would expect between 60% and 90% of the wood produced from clear felling to go as timber with only the tops and branches being left as firewood. It is clearly most important that the clear felled area is relatively small in relation to the size of the forest or woodland. It is also vital that the forester pays close attention to how this bare area is then regenerated with young trees.

Trees are clear felled at economic maturity but they have many productive years before this and to prevent overcrowding a forester generally undertakes several thinning operations. This is the process where unwanted trees are removed every 5 to 10 years to allow the others the light and space to grow on. Thinning produces a great deal of firewood, which the forester is usually happy to sell, although the operation is generally expensive with costs barely covered by income.

Many species of broadleaf tree and all of the firewood species will regrow from a cut stump and this characteristic is used to re-generate woodland in the ancient practice of coppicing. This tech-nique was probably developed way back in the early Bronze Age, in fact as soon as man had acquired reasonably efficient cutting tools. Coppicing may even be earlier than this as there is some evidence of coppiced hazel being used to form Stone Age walkways across peaty or marshy land. Whatever its origins coppicing is probably the most widely used management system in our smaller broadleaved wood-lands. The length of time between each cut varies depending on the tree species and the type of material being grown. Hazel grown for pea sticks, bean poles fencing and hedging material may be cut every 6 to 8 years. Ash or alder being grown for firewood may be cut every 20 to 30 years and the slower growing oak say every 30 to 40 years. While a few conifer species will coppice these are rarer trees and it is fair to say that conifers are never commercially coppiced.

For woodland harvesting to be truly sustainable it is absolutely vital that the felled trees are replaced by young growth. With clear felling this is usually achieved by planting little tree seedlings, which have been grown in forest nurseries. Alternatively, if there are mature trees of a suitable species around the clear felled area, some foresters

▶    TOP LEFT A rural craftsman making a traditional split hazel hurdle.

▶    TOP RIGHT A rural craftsman splitting hazel rod for hurdle making using a bill hook.

▶    Bundles of prepared hazel rods at the roadside.

let mother nature take her course and the area is naturally regenerated with seed from these mature trees. With coppicing, the forester only needs to prevent the young regrowth from being eaten by deer, rabbits or hare.

In Britain forest and woodland management is a mature and well regulated industry. From small privately owned woodlands to the vast forest blocks managed by the Forestry Commission, over 99% of the trees are cared for and felled trees replaced. Those interested in the future of our trees and the production of firewood can have confidence that the balance essential to the well being of our woodlands is being well maintained and the timber and firewood harvested is being sustainably produced.

## Types of wood fuel

Wood fuel comes in a number of different forms, the most common of which is the firewood log, but there are also wood pellets, woodchips, manufactured logs and kindling.

Firewood logs – The simplest form of wood fuel where the trunk and branches of a tree are cross-cut into short lengths usually between 9 and 12 inches long. It is important to know the maximum length of log that your wood burning stove can take and buy or cut your wood accordingly. However it's easier to make and maintain a good fire with a variety of log sizes so always try to ensure you have a good mixture available for burning in your wood store.

Firewood kindling – The ancient word 'kindling' describes the little sticks used to start a fire and get it going. Kindling can simply be small dry sticks gathered from a hedgerow or wood chopped into small pieces of roughly ½ – 1 inch diameter. Knot free conifer logs are most commonly used to make kindling, with pine being among the most popular species. Wood recovered during building renovation or from old pallets is often used to make kindling, although care needs to be taken during sawing to miss any screws or nails still in the wood.

◀ TOP Cross-cutting sweet chestnut coppice.

◀ BOTTOM Using horses to haul logs from woodland is now becoming more popular as they cause less damage.

**Wood pellets** – As we've detailed in Chapter One, pellet stoves are gaining in popularity and use a reconstituted wood fuel made either from pulverised wood or from wood waste extruded into small pellets. The quality of wood pellets varies but, in general, they offer a fuel that is clean, easy to move around, and relatively low in moisture content. Against these advantages, the simple fact that wood pellets are a heavily processed wood fuel generally makes them more expensive weight for weight than wood logs.

**Wood briquettes** – Made by the same process as wood pellets, the briquettes are extruded into cylinders around 50mm to 75mm in diameter and 150mm to 300mm long. To all intents and purposes, they are manufactured to resemble natural logs.

**Wood chips** – Unlike wood pellets, wood chips are less heavily processed than wood pellets and are best suited to larger automated wood boilers of the type used to heat very large homes, schools, hospitals and, at the industrial level, wood-fuelled power stations. Wood chips are hugely important in terms of our move towards using wood as a source of renewable energy but are of very limited interest to the owner of a modern wood burning stove.

## Buying firewood

In many ways buying firewood is the single most important part of owning a wood burning stove. Getting this right will lead to your stove being a source of comfort and pleasure; getting it wrong can make your life a nightmare!

Although buying wood fuel is different from buying electricity, gas, oil and coal, there are now a number of recognised wood fuel quality schemes that include all the leading producers and suppliers. These accredited producers or suppliers have to demonstrate compliance with recognised quality standards, which also consider the source and sustainability of the wood products they sell.

HETAS, the government recognised body that promotes the safe

◀ Loose logs, dry kilned logs, wood briquettes and kindling.

and effective use of solid fuel and biomass, including wood fuels and related technologies. HETAS has a comprehensive web site **www. hetas.co.uk** and publishes an annual guide of approved products and services. Both the website and guide include a comprehensive directory of accredited wood fuel producers and suppliers.

Historically firewood was sold by the 'cord', a cord being the amount of branch wood that, when well stacked, would occupy an overall volume of 128 ft$^3$. The wood was stacked as tightly as possible so that small mammals could not crawl between the logs. The length of logs varies by country and region. A well stacked cord with an overall volume of 128 ft$^3$ could contain the equivalent of up to 75ft$^3$ of solid wood depending on the straightness of the wood and the quality of stacking. Although it may still be possible to buy a cord of firewood from a traditional woodland estate, it is more likely that you will be offered either a stack of firewood measured in cubic metres or a load of cut logs.

As a general rule it is preferable to buy your wood by volume than by weight. The volume of wood varies very little as it dries but its weight varies hugely as freshly cut logs usually contain at least 50% water. If you choose to buy logs by weight, it is important that you get some assurance or guarantee of their moisture content. With the growing interest in wood burning, specialised suppliers have entered the market with several of them offering logs that have been kiln or air dried to reduce their moisture content. Buying dried logs means you pretty well know how much energy you are buying and, just as importantly, your wood fuel is immediately ready to use.

Wood can be bought in various ways including from the back of a truck or trailer pre-packed bags and in so shop around to ensure the wood you are buying, comes from a reliable source and is not simply the spoils of local one-off tree destruction resulting from road or building works. It's a good idea to make the seller aware of your investment in a wood burning stove and that you will be buying firewood for many years. Building a relationship with a firewood supplier is key to ensuring a regular, reliable source of quality firewood. You can look for firewood merchants using the normal channels, ad-

▲ Radial cracks showing on logs.

vertisements in the local paper or nowadays on the internet, but don't forget to ask around among those who are already burning logs for their recommendations. For even more peace of mind, try and visit your intended supplier to see how the wood is handled, cut and seasoned.

We look at seasoning later on, but for now it is important for you to know exactly what volume is being offered at what price and whether the wood is freshly cut or if it has been seasoned, and if so for how long. With experience you will learn to look at logs and instantly judge how well seasoned they are. Is the bark cracking and falling off, have radial cracks developed on the cut ends, has any wood exposed to sunlight turned grey, and do the logs feel light or heavy? Moisture meters are now readily available and fairly cheap and it is probably a good idea in the early days to buy one and use it to help you build up the experience you need.

Freshly cut wet wood is usually around 50% moisture content

which, with kiln or air drying (seasoning), should be brought down to 20 – 25%. When using your moisture meter make sure you test several different logs, even asking for one or two to be split so that you can test the freshly cut surface. The moisture content within a load of logs can vary widely depending on species and where in the wood stack the individual logs have laid. It is therefore important that you test enough logs to give yourself some idea what the average moisture content is.

Lastly, be sure to discuss delivery. How does the supplier deliver, when can they deliver, will they simply tip the logs in your drive or are they able to reach your wood store? How far will they deliver and is delivery free or are they looking to charge you extra for this service?

Bags of firewood logs are often sold in garage forecourts but only consider buying this wood if it is clearly branded and from a known and reliable supplier. Often the logs found on garage forecourts are from unseasoned conifer, which will burn poorly, can be very expensive and is not good for the life of your stove.

## The Small Woods Association

The Small Woods Association supports the sustainable management of woodlands and the production and marketing of wood products for local markets. It provides services to woodland owners, practitioners and producers and aims to signpost anyone interested in local woods to local groups who encourage access, make products, and provide services or training.

It provides input to policy forums and lobbies at all levels to promote the wellbeing of small woodlands and all those who own, manage or work in them. Services include a quarterly magazine for owners and those with a general interest in making better use of UK woods, and a twice yearly practitioner's magazine for those with a more professional interest.

The Small Woods Association offers an enquiries service for those who need help or local contacts and arranges training, meetings, local networks seminars and woodland visits for members. It delivers many services through woodland projects, including the Woodland Initiatives Network, the National Coppice Restoration Project, Heartwoods, Coed Lleol, Herefordshire Sustain, forest schools, volunteering and social forestry projects in Hereford, Shropshire and Telford. For further information visit **www.smallwoods.org.uk**.

## Gathering firewood

This is a huge subject but perhaps the most important point is the simple one that you just can't pick up wood you see beside the road or anywhere else without clearing it with the owner first.

A small pile of logs beside the road where somebody has been doing some work on a power line or overhanging trees may sit there for weeks but they still belong to somebody. In Britain we have the common right to gather some forms of wild food to feed our families, for instance wild mushrooms and blackberries, but this right does not extend to wood fuel. The exception to this rule is in the rare cases where an ancient right to gather fuel wood exists and applies to an individual property, a group of houses or sometimes an entire village. If you are uncertain whether or not your property enjoys such rights, the local parish council should be able to advise you.

In recent years there has been a rise in interest from people wanting to own a small woodland. These woodlands only come to the market occasionally and nowadays command a high price per acre. Further information is available via The Small Woods Association. A much older group, the Royal Forestry Society (**www.rfs.org.uk**), while dealing mainly with large private estates also welcomes owners of small woodlands.

Owning your own woodland is the ultimate solution to the need to have a wood supply but there are still some rules governing aspects of management and how much wood you can cut each year. For those people who already own woodland, or are thinking of buying one, the critical question is how much woodland you need to be able to harvest enough firewood, sustainably, to keep your home warm. A very broad rule of thumb is that broadleaved woodland grows about

▲ A chain saw operative wearing the appropriate safety equipment.

$3m^3$ to $4m^3$ of wood per hectare per year. There is a huge variation in woodland productivity depending on the tree species involved, the soil type, rainfall and altitude. It used to be said that if a farmer had 20 acres of woodland he could keep his farmhouse warm all year (a hectare is 2.47 acres).

As the owner of a wood burning stove, you will quickly develop an eye for every twig, branch or scrap piece of wood that you think you can burn. While scrap wood will seldom be enough to meet your annual needs, it can make a contribution. Don't be surprised to find yourself looking in skips to see how much wood someone has thrown away; if you see a tree surgeon at work, ask him what he's going to do with the logs or branch wood. Remind your neighbours of your interest in wood.

▲　LEFT An example of a log splitting axe. RIGHT An example of a hand axe.

## Safety comes first

If you own or are going to buy woodland and intend to do the harvesting work yourself you are very strongly advised to get professional chainsaw training. Chainsaws in well trained hands are safe and efficient tools, chainsaws in untrained hands are potentially lethal. Although easy to use, the misuse of axes and saws can also lead to injury so get some basic training in their use, keep all your tools out of the reach of small children, and always take a first aid box with you when working away from your home or vehicle. Finally, wear the correct protective clothing. Rubber gardening gloves will afford you little or no protection when using a chainsaw and eye protection is essential. As you will have seen when watching contractors prune or remove trees, today's health and safety rules require the use of hard hats, all round eye protection, proper clothing and, for higher work, safety harnesses and ropes.

## Burning recovered or scrap wood

Having mentioned the amount of wood that is wasted each year it is only right to consider a few points of caution before you consider collecting and burning it. Scrap wood may well contain old nails, screws and possibly shards of glass if the wood has come from window frames. The wood may have had some form of treatment – paint, creosote or other anti-fungal or anti-wood-boring insect preservatives. Before handling or using any of this wood try and find out its history, and, if it was treated, what exactly that treatment was.

As a general rule it is better to avoid any wood that has been treated with preservatives. Some of the insecticides used in the past were highly toxic and included organochlorines. Fungicides too contained highly toxic chemicals such as arsenic.

Although these toxic components become stable salts when used in wood treatment, they may become unstable when roasted in a fire. Wood treated with creosote, wood tar or some of the earlier wood preservatives is usually more flammable than natural wood and can burn out of control in a wood stove. If you are uncertain if scrap wood is safe to burn, the simple rule is don't use it.

## The best woods to burn

In truth, it makes little difference which species of tree is the source of the wood logs for your stove although it makes a great deal of difference if you're burning wood on an open fire.

Seasoning the logs is far more important than knowing which tree they have come from and most wood burning stoves are remarkably tolerant. Nonetheless it may be of interest to have some understanding of the nature and characteristics of the primary broadleaved trees and the subtle differences in how their wood burns.

The ancient rhyme that follows, while referring to open fires, has some merit although it does give elm an undeservedly bad name!

An ancient ryhme

> Beechwood fires are bright and clear,
> If the logs are kept a year.
> Chestnut's only good, they say,
> If for long it's laid away.
> Birch and fir logs burn too fast,
> Blaze up bright and do not last.
> Elm wood burns like a churchyard mould,
> Even the very flames are cold.
> Poplar gives a bitter smoke,
> Fills your eyes and makes you choke.
> Apple wood will scent your room
> With an incense-like perfume.
> Oak and maple, if dry and old,
> Keep away the winter cold.
> But ash wood wet and ash wood dry,
> A King shall warm his slippers by.

The primary characteristics of the ten most common firewood trees are as follows;

**Alder** – A tree most commonly found on wet ground and by streams and rivers. It grows quickly and burns well; it is also very easy to split. The freshly cut wood is white, but this soon turns to a dark orange, which readily identifies alder among other logs. Alder firewood is often produced during work to improve riverbanks.

**Ash** – A tree with delicate foliage easily identified by its ash grey bark and large bunches of seeds, called keys. Ash firewood is highly prized as it is very easy to split and will burn even when freshly cut. A great deal of ash firewood is produced from thinnings, but it will also re-grow, as coppice.

**Beech** – This large, shady tree's wood is best known for fine furniture and flooring and provides first-class firewood. Beech firewood mostly comes from thinnings or as branch wood from felled mature trees, it does not coppice well.

**Birch** – Some say our most beautiful tree and often called 'the lady of the woods'. It makes excellent firewood and is the primary fuel in many northern parts of Europe. Birch splits well but is apt to rot very quickly so extra care should be taken during seasoning. Its wood smoke is particularly aromatic.

**Elm** – A much underrated wood, now scarce due to Dutch elm disease. Even the old rhymes advise against using this wood. It is very hard to split and slow to dry, but for providing a hearth of glowing embers there is nothing better. Elm firewood is primarily taken from hedgerows where the disease has killed the young trees and these dead trees have then been allowed to stand until the bark falls off.

**Oak** – This is perhaps the most majestic and well known of all our trees. Once famous for shipbuilding and now for house building, furniture and flooring, the oak provides excellent firewood. The firewood is usually cut from the branches of felled mature trees, although it does coppice well. As a general rule freshly cut oak firewood should be seasoned for two years as it is very slow to dry. If you need a shorter seasoning period the logs should be split into small pieces, say 3 inches diameter, which can then be ready to burn after one summer.

Sycamore – A tree of mixed reputation, which is strong in the face of winter gales and provides welcome shade on hot summer days. It acts as a host to millions of aphids each spring when the leaves produce a mass of honeydew, which then becomes sooty with mildew and falls onto whatever is beneath the tree. Parking beneath a sycamore is not recommended! The firewood of sycamore is easy to split and dry and is mostly produced during thinning operations. It coppices well and is a member of the maple family.

**Thorn and fruit tree wood** – Thorn or fruit tree firewood is possibly the best firewood of all. Hawthorn, apple and pear all burn really well, giving excellent embers and a wonderfully scented wood smoke. Hawthorn will burn when still 'green' (unseasoned).

Willow and poplar – Wide-spread and fast-growing but make poor firewood. The wood will burn in a wood stove but it's advisable to burn it in mixture with better burning woods.

Hardwoods make better fuel for stoves than softwoods (like conifers and spruce). Many types of softwood contain resin and burn poorly unless very well seasoned. If you are going to burn softwoods, season them for two years after splitting. If you have a small quantity of relatively knot-free conifer this may be best cut into kindling.

## The seasoning process

An odd word 'seasoning', much more widely used by cooks wishing to improve the palatability of a meal by the addition of salt and pepper! With firewood however, the word 'seasoning' is used more like a dark art. Countrymen can talk and argue for hours about the seasoning of firewood, the needs of each species and whether or not to split the wood. Why, if a wood will burn when it's green do we need to season at all? How many years does it take for oak to season? What do they do with conifers?

As with most aspects of woodland management and the production, handling and burning of firewood there are very few absolute rights and wrongs.

When used in connection with firewood the word 'seasoning' simply means drying. Unlike wine, logs do not improve by maturing or ageing – seasoning is simply drying the logs. This drying process is complicated by the structure of the wood and bark, and by the fact that we are not simply removing water. Tree sap will always contain a wide range of dissolved mineral salts and in certain species and at certain times of the year the sap may have a high content of sugars. These compounds are hygroscopic, that is they will absorb water, and this to some extent makes drying firewood a little like trying to dry clothes or a towel that is wet with seawater. The fluids within coniferous timber are even more complicated.

There are a few tree species where the wood will burn 'green' (freshly cut and unseasoned) and although you will still meet people who insist that ash, hawthorn and furze burn just as well green as seasoned, seasoning any wood will be beneficial. Burning 'green' wood should really only ever be done as a last resort because it's the least efficient way of burning wood. Imagine a firewood log has 10 units of heat energy trapped in it which can be released as heat to warm your home. If the log is completely dry, most of the trapped energy is released as heat, but if it's damp some of the heat generated in the fire will be used to dry out the wood as it burns.

So, if you are persuaded to the advantages of seasoning, how should you handle and treat your wood logs?

Later we look at the basic design of a woodshed but, for now, let's look at the pre-storage preparation of the logs themselves. A log in the round has two cut ends and is otherwise encased in tree bark, which we know is largely waterproof. We can hugely improve the drying process if we split the log into one or more pieces before storing it in the woodshed. A split log has a much greater surface area available to dry from and the cut bark is more likely to peel back and come loose.

Sometimes logs that are not split never seem to dry out. This may be due to each cut end drying a little and shrinking and sealing in the remaining moisture, which cannot escape through the intact waterproof bark.

So, for the quickest and most effective seasoning any log with a diameter greater than 4 inches should be split before storing. The length of time it takes to season the logs will vary depending on the tree species, the size of the logs and which part of Britain you live in. Let's deal with tree species first.

Oak needs at least one and up to two years of seasoning before burning. Traditional saw millers cutting oak planks and beams reckoned to give a piece of oak a year of air-drying for every inch of thickness although they were as much concerned with splitting and warping as the actual drying.

With the exception of oak, almost all of the other broadleaf tree species can be grouped together under the general advice of cutting this winter for burning next winter. This means the logs will have been harvested when the trees are dormant and contain relatively little sap and will then have the entire spring, summer and autumn to dry out.

You may live in an area where there is an abundance of conifer forest and a proportion of your firewood may come from these conifers. In the same way as the word 'broadleaved' covers all of our oaks, beech, birch, maples, etc the word 'conifer' groups together our pines, firs, spruce, larch, hemlocks, cedars, etc. Some conifers such as pine are particularly resinous; others such as hemlock seem particularly wet. The best working practice is probably to aim to season freshly cut conifer logs for at least two years.

Although the best advice is to use conifer as little as possible and buy broadleaf firewood whenever you can, for one resident of Wales, conifer is a favourite.

## Splitting logs

There are three ways to split a log: by using a simple and old-fashioned axe, a sledge hammer and wedges, or a hydraulic ram. Let's start with a splitting axe (including the splitting mauls specifically designed for difficult logs). If you are going to use an axe it should have a good strong handle, be heavy enough – say four pounds or more and, ironically, relatively blunt. When splitting wood with a sharp axe it can frequently jam without splitting the log.

Practise at hitting the same spot on a log time after time and you can settle into a steady, rhythmic, pattern of log splitting. Never rush or try to work too quickly. Work steadily at a pace that leaves you out of breath. In this way you may be able to work for a few hours without really tiring and split a large stack of wood! Stay safe by keeping the area you are standing in clear of split wood and do not let anybody who is watching or helping you come anywhere near you while you are splitting. Occasionally you will misjudge a log and the axe may ricochet with the risk of injury to anyone close. Also resist the temptation to wear gloves when working with an axe. You need a good grip and to feel the axe shaft; wearing gloves will inhibit this and make your work clumsier. If possible do not work in the rain when the axe handle and logs are wet. Everything just gets slippery and you are much more likely to have an accident.

Choose your chopping block carefully. You will need a fairly large, tough log on which to split all your other firewood logs. The best chopping blocks are made from the lowest part of the tree trunk (the stump), the very first part of the tree that is above ground. A chopping block made from a tree stump will almost always have some buttressing, where it widens out in contact with the roots and the wood fibres are matted, making it much more difficult to split.

If you choose to work with a sledgehammer and wedges the basic skills required are very similar to those needed for axe work. You

▶   TOP Logs before splitting and processed logs behind.
▶   MIDDLE Examples of different types of axes.
▶   BOTTOM Hydraulic ram log splitter.

probably still have a chopping block and your swing with the sledge-hammer needs to be accurate enough to hit the wedge cleanly. You can buy wedges that are specifically designed for splitting firewood logs, they are round or star shaped cones. A word of caution – hitting an iron or steel wedge with an iron sledgehammer is dangerous as tiny splinters of iron can fly out like pieces of shrapnel so, to minimise the risk of eye injury, wear protective goggles and use wedges made of nylon or a soft magnesium alloy which do not splinter.

If you do not want to use an axe or sledge hammer, or expect to be working with large knotty logs that will be hard to split, you should consider one of the many styles of hydraulic ram system that are currently on the market. These machines take all of the hard work out of log splitting by driving a wedge slowly into the log, which is held in place by a metal frame. The force of these machines is so great that even the most difficult log splits under this treatment.

Woodsmen tend to split logs to patterns that will then give a good variety of shapes and sizes to burn, which also helps stacking in the woodshed. Small logs are usually left whole or split in half; larger logs are split into four or six segments.

## Storing firewood

The two essential rules when seasoning your firewood are to keep the rain off the logs and to allow a good airflow through them. By far the best way of achieving this is to erect a purpose-made woodshed. Some people are tempted to put their freshly delivered logs into the corner of an almost airtight garden shed or damp outbuilding and close the door. At best these logs will dry very slowly and at worst they may even rot.

In the overall planning to fit a wood burning stove you should carefully consider where you intend to store your wood and the space it will require if, for example, you're going store two years' worth of firewood.

### Woodshed construction

It is always better to build a woodshed that is slightly bigger than you think you need. Best of all is a woodshed with two primary bays, one for the wood that you are currently using and the other for the wood that you are seasoning ready for use next winter. Trying to manage the seasoning and storing of your firewood in a small woodshed is very difficult as in practice it is hard to segregate the fresh logs from those which have been in the woodshed for some time. A woodshed needs to be little more than a roof with three slatted sides. The front is open for easy working both within the shed and for unloading and stacking the logs – stacked firewood takes up significantly less room than firewood just thrown in a heap.

### Wood stacking

How you stack your firewood is important as not only is it a way of maximising your use of space but it should also make the wood stack safe and prevent logs falling down when you're collecting fresh supplies. Stacking firewood logs is a little like dry stonewalling, every log is a different size or shape and you must think how best it fits into the stack you are making. Use the big, heavy, split logs to make the corners interlocking them and using their weight to make the corner stable. Laying the logs on the edges of the wood stack (the outside wall) so that they are slightly sloping downwards and outwards allows them to shed any rain and prevent it from entering the stack. Ancient dry stone buildings were made like this; the stones lay sloping slightly outwards to prevent the rain from entering the building.

Site the woodshed not only for good airflow but somewhere where it will also get some sun and not under trees or over hanging buildings. Your woodshed should have a base to prevent the firewood from lying in contact with bar earth as any logs touching the ground will absorb moisture which could promote rotting. A firm, dry base of concrete is fine but make sure there is some slope so that puddles do not form beneath the logs. A free-draining base may be best and this could be either stout paving slabs on sand or coarse gravel (say 1–2 inches, 25–50mm). In both cases make sure that they

are resting on a tough permeable membrane. This will prevent soil from migrating into the sand or gravel and reducing its drying effectiveness, it will also help to prevent weed growth. Any weeds in or around your woodshed will slow airflow and reduce the shed's effectiveness; for drying logs.

A tarpaulin can be used as a temporary measure to store and protect firewood or if space is really limited. However a great deal of wood is ruined by poor use of tarpaulins so only use one as a temporary store and again ensure the logs are not in direct contact with the ground by providing a suitable base, which could, for example, be made of pallets.

The tarpaulin you buy should be of good quality; once the wood is stacked on its base, the tarpaulin should be pulled tightly over the logs and secured against the wind. Using bricks on the top and side often creates puddles so, using the eyelets around the edges of the tarpaulin, tie it down much as you would a tent in stormy weather. Do not bring the sides right down to the ground, to ensure air can still flow freely through your wood pile.

## Laying and lighting your stove

There are three stages in lighting and successfully burning wood logs in your new stove. The first is the obvious one of actually getting the fire lit and going well. The second stage is maintaining the fire to give the amount of heat that you want during the hours that you have it alight. The last stage, and just as important as the first two, is deciding how you are going to let the fire die down and eventually die out.

Before you start ensure you have everything to hand to light the fire and get it burning well. You will need paper, kindling, matches and wood logs. Firelighters can be a great help and several types are now on the market including some made from wax coated wood shavings.

◀ A typical woodshed showing good air flow.

### Stage one

Arrange three or four logs in a well spaced triangle or square inside the stove leaving a clear space in the middle. If you're using split logs that still have some bark on them, position the split surfaces towards the middle of the triangle or square and the surfaces with bark towards the outside of the stove.

Screw up two or three small pieces of newspaper into tight balls and place in the middle of the triangle or square and lay dry kindling over the paper in a criss cross pattern leaving enough space to get a match to the paper. Alternatively, substitute firelighters for the newspaper and continue as before.

Light the newspaper in two separate places and once the flames become established add further kindling without smothering the fire. Once you can see that the kindling is well alight lay smaller logs on top, again being careful to neither smother nor starve this baby fire. By the time these smaller logs are burning the larger outer logs should be burning too – your fire is now alight.

It is a good idea to give the freshly lit fire plenty of air and fuel but as stove designs vary significantly, read the manufacturer's instructions to determine the best way of controlling the air flow while lighting the fire. Remember that an important element of a good stove fire is getting the chimney or flue to a temperature that pulls air through the stove, so it may be wise to minimise the time the door of the stove is open during lighting.

Once alight with the first charge of logs burning well and glowing embers accumulating at the base of the fire, it's time to move to the next stage.

### Stage two

Once securely alight you need to give your stove enough fuel and air to maintain the burning rate you need to be comfortable. This may be a really good blaze for a freezing winter's day or a steady tick-over sufficient to keep the chill off the room.

A well proven trick is to add new logs just before they seem to be needed. If you let the fire get too low you may need to resort to kindling again to get it going. Never push the new logs into the embers; try and lay them with a tiny gap, say half an inch, above the embers. This allows the new logs enough air to start burning easily. Another habit some people have is to keep giving the burning logs a good poking! This is a leftover from the days of open coal fires where poor quality fuel had to be stirred up with a poker to allow air in and keep it burning brightly. You almost never need to do this with a wood fire and it will disturb and disrupt a well burning fire.

Assuming you are not intending to burn your stove overnight, you need to think about extinguishing it about an hour before you intend to leave it.

### Stage three

You should never simply abandon a fire without careful thought on how it should continue burning until it goes out. Do you want it to simply peter out, or is it a freezing cold night and you want it to burn for as long as possible?

If you are happy to let the fire die out as the fuel runs out, experience will soon tell you how long it takes the logs you last added to burn away. Remember there are no hard and fast rules about how much fuel you should add when the stove needs refueling so the number and size of the logs you add will pretty much control the time it takes to burn down.

If you want the stove to be burning for some time long after you've left it, this requires a little more planning. A common and fundamental mistake is to load the fire with fresh logs and reduce the air supply just before retiring. The fire may burn slowly for many hours, but with the temperature much lower than normal it is likely to accelerate the formation of tars, creosote and acidic pyrogenous liquids that can condense in the chimney.

As an alternative, make the last charge of logs a really big one at least half an hour before you intend leaving the fire. Give the fire plenty of air to help build up enough heat to burn off the flammable volatiles and only then reduce the air and leave the fire. The logs should be half embers before you turn the air down and will then smoulder on well into the night without problems.

An important difference between wood and coal fires is how one treats the ash. With coal fires it is important to remove the ash and clinker every day. The ash content of wood is much less than coal and so it needs to be cleaned out less frequently, but there is a more important consideration. Wood fires work best on a bed of glowing embers where they will glow away giving lots of heat for hours. Only clear out the minimum of ash and only when absolutely necessary as a new fire will be easier to light if bedded on the ash of previous fires.

## Tree and woodland regulations

The trees and woodlands of Britain are generally managed to the highest standards and are supported by officers working for county councils, local authorities and, most importantly, the Forestry Commission. The woodland officers working for the Forestry Commission are in place to oversee the management of our woodlands through the government's system of grants and felling licences and are an excellent source of information should you need some help or advice.

If you intend to fell a tree, or trees, it is always best to check first whether the tree is in a conservation area or may be subject to a tree preservation order. Even if neither of these apply you may still require a felling licence from the Forestry Commission. Felling licences are required following simple, sensible legislation which came into being after the second world war to control the overall amount of tree felling in Britain. Cutting a small amount of firewood is generally allowed without a licence but it's worth checking with your local woodland officer before you start any work.

**MORE THAN JUST A STOVE!**

# Heat the house not just the room!

**BUY BRITISH**

Highly Commended

◊ Makes a huge saving against your gas or oil heating bills.
◊ Burns wood logs.
◊ One charge of 10kg logs heats the appliance to full heat, to release that heat for 12 hours after fire has gone out.
◊ 25% of stored heat still released after 12hrs [model 678 shown above].
◊ No ducting or water connections needed—just leave your doors open to allow heat to circulate (does not overheat the room it stands in).
◊ Made in England, HETAS approved and DEFRA exempt for inner city installations
◊ Four models in the range.
◊ All colour options available.

## Email—sales@landyvent.co.uk
## Call Landy Vent UK Ltd—01527 857814
### Ask about our new E730 oval model just released!
www.eccostove.com

See page 30 for further details of Silicon Carbide, Masonry and Kachelofen heaters

# flue&ducting

## Flue and Chimney Supplies

# ◉ DINAK

FLUE & DUCTING IS AN OFFICIAL STOCKIST OF DINAK MODULAR CHIMNEY SYSTEMS

**Call now to open your account and receive an extra 10% off your first Dinak order. Just quote coupon Ref: DINAK13**

**Next day delivery as standard. Same day delivery is available on request**

Trade Counter Opening Hours

**Monday - Friday - 8am to 5pm**

Flue & Ducting Ltd
Herrod Avenue, Whitehill Industrial Estate, Reddish, SK4 1NU,

**To order please call:** 0161 480 2994
**Email:** sales@flue-ducting.co.uk
or collect from our trade counter

# CERTAINLY™ WOOD

## SUSTAINABLE
# BRITISH
## WOOD FUEL

- PREMIER BRITISH KILN-DRIED WOOD FUEL
- CARBON NEUTRAL FUELS FROM WOOD-FIRED KILNS
- LOCALLY SOURCED
- NEW WOODLAND CREATION
- FAMILY BUSINESS

### Why kiln-dried?

- LESS MOISTURE = MORE HEAT
- MORE HEAT = LESS WOOD
- LESS SOOT AND TAR
- A CLEANER BURN

**fuelled by nature**

HETAS

# THE DIRECTORY

The list of suppliers detailed in the following pages have been compiled from both *The Official Guide to HETAS Approved Products and Services List no 19, 2013* (in which case a HETAS logo is shown) and on the recommendations of our editors. The directory, due to space constraints, only deals with certain models and the publishers have tried to ensure that the information is as up-to-date and accurate at the time of going to press in August 2013.

To determine the heat output that your stove should be, there are a number of issues to think about. Firstly the manufacturer's instructions should be read as there may be specific guidance provided. The following guideline is rough, is for guidance only, and should be backed up with a site survey. The table below is based on a 'typical' single living room, a room with with two external walls, two windows and a room above and a room above. If open stairways or other rooms lead from the room with the stove then you will probably need to choose a higher output. Always take professional advice.

Approximate room volume length x width x height

| Property Type | 30m³ | 40m³ | 50m³ | 60m³ | 70m³ | 80m³ | 90m³ |
|---|---|---|---|---|---|---|---|
| Older/poorly insulated pre 1950's | 3.3kW | 4.3kW | 5 kW | 6 kW | 6.5 kW | 7.2 kW | 8.1 kW |
| Moderately insulated properties 1990's | | 2.4 kW | 2.8 kW | 3.3 kW | 3.8 kW | 4.2 kW | 4.6 kW |
| Modern well insulated post 2008 | | | | 2.3 kW | 2.6 kW | 3.0 kw | 3.2 kW |

*Reproduced with kind permission of HETAS*

# AGA RANGEMASTER

From its ever popular Little Wenlock Classic which is perfect for the smaller home to its Minsterley model - which has a boiler for hot water and powering radiators, there is an AGA wood-burning stove to suit every home and budget. And for urban and city centre dwellers there is also a smoke-exempt version of the Little Wenlock Classic to comply with the stringent clean air regulations.

Model: **Little Wenlock**
Rated output kW: **5.0**
UK distributor: **AGA Rangemaster**
Address: **Station Road, Ketle, Telford, Shropshire, TF1 5AQ**
Tel: **0845 381365**
Website: **www.agaliving.com**

Model: **Ludlow**
Rated output kW: **6.6**
UK distributor: **AGA Rangemaster**
Address: **Station Road, Ketle, Telford, Shropshire, TF1 5AQ**
Tel: **0845 381365**
Website: **www.agaliving.com**

# AMESTI

Amesti stoves are developed in Chile, a heavily wooded country where reliance on wood fired heating for 6-9 months of the year is the norm. To comply with Chilean air quality regulations, which have one of the strictest particulate emission thresholds in the world, Amesti developed an exceptional clean combustion system which is used in their Nordic stoves.

Model: **Nordic 350**
Rated output kW: **7.3**
UK distributor: **Gardeco**
Address: **PO Box 5500,**
**Kiderminster, DY11 9BB**
Tel: **0870 2340003**
Website: **www.gardeco.co.uk**

**HETAS**

**Other models available**
Model: **Nordic 360**
Rated output kW: **8.5**

Model: **Nordic 380**
Rated output kW: **10.2**

Model: **Nordic 450**
Rated output kW: **14.0**

# AQUATHERM

Aquatherm Eco stoves are a range of contemporary, high quality woodburning insert stoves with boilers big enough to heat your whole house. Aquatherm Eco stoves all have large, airwashed windows, with flat, curved or panoramic models available. These doors open by sliding up and into the wall above or some that hinge outwards into the room.

Model: **Eco F21 with boiler**
Rated output kW: **10. 5 for water**
and **4.5 to the room**
UK distributor: **Aquatherm**
Address: **Capton, Devon, TQ6 OJE**
Tel: **0844 3320155**
Website: **www. aquathermstoves. co.uk**

Model: **Eco F34 with boiler**
Rated output kW: **24.0 for water**
and **10.0 to the room**
UK distributor: **Aquatherm**
Address: **Capton, Devon, TQ6 OJE**
Tel: **0844 3320155**
Website: **www. aquathermstoves. co.uk**

# ARADA

Arada has been at the forefront of innovations in wood burning stoves for several decades. All Arada stoves are manufactured in a purpose-built factory in the heart of the Devon countryside. They work closely with carefully selected suppliers to ensure that only the finest raw materials go into their products. They produce stoves under various trade names including Aarow, Hamlet, Stratford and Villager.

Model: **Aarow Acorn 5**
Rated output kW: **5.0**
UK distributor: **Arada Ltd**
Address: **The Fireworks, Weycroft Avenue, Axminster, Devon, EX13 5HU**
Tel: **01297 357000**
Website: **www.arada.uk.com**

Model: **Aarow Ecoburn 7**
Rated output kW: **6.0**
UK distributor: **Arada Ltd**
Address: **The Fireworks, Weycroft Avenue, Axminster, Devon, EX13 5HU**
Tel: **01297 357000**
Website: **www.arada.uk.com**

HETAS

129

# ARKIANE

Arkiane was founded in 1990 by Dominique Lelong, a true fireplace professional, and many customers have put their trust in his products. The company's activities include: conception and creation of new fireplace models, client advisory service, production management, custom designed installation plans, order processing and on-site installation. The Kephren stove has four tubes hidden behind the cover's stiles which draw the smoke and evacuate it by a horizontal tube linked to a vertical chimney.

Model: **Kephren**
Rated output kW: **12.0**
UK distributor: **Arkiane stoves are available from a number of retailers including Stovesonline**
Address: **Capton, Dartmouth, Devon, TQ6 OJE**
Tel: **0845 226 5754**
Website: **www. stovesonline.co.uk**

# BFM EUROPE

Portway stoves date back to the 1800's and were named 'Tortoise' as they burned 'slow but sure'. Today all Portway multifuel stoves carry independently tested CE approval to standard BS EN 13240 and are so efficient and clean burning they have received Defra's recommendation for exemption from the Clean Air Act 1993. Portway stoves which carry this symbol can be used in Smoke Control Areas when burning wood, as well as authorised smokeless fuels.

Model: **Portway 2**
Rated output kW: **7.0**
UK distributor: **BFM Europe**
Address: **Gordon Banks Drive, Trentham Lakes, Stoke-on-Trent, Staffordshire ST4 4TJ**
Tel: **01782 339000**
Website: **www. bfm-europe.com**

**Other models available**
Model: **Portway 1**
Rated output kW: **5.0**

Model: **Portway 3**
Rated output kW: **9.0**

Model: **Portway Marine**
Rated output kW: **4.8**

# BROSLEY

Brosley produce Defra approved woodburning stoves as well as pellet and biomass appliances. The models in the Broseley Fires range are available in multifuel, wood burning, electric and gas fuel versions. In the UK, they have pioneered the Safety Cold Water System woodburning boiler stoves which are capable of being run on sealed heating systems rather than conventional vented heating systems.

Model: **Hercules**
Rated output kW: **12.0**
UK distributor: **Brosley Fires Ltd**
Address: **Knights Way, Battlefield Enterprise Park, Shrewsbury, Shropshire, SY1 3AB**
Tel: **01743 461444**
Website: **www.brosleyfires.com**

**Other models available**
Model: **Serrano 3**
Rated output kW: **3**

Model: **Winchester**
Rated output kW: **8.0**

Model: **York Grande SE**
Rated output kW: **7.0**

Model: **Snowdon with boiler**
Rated output kW: **22 to water and 8.0 to room**

# CAPITAL FIREPLACES

Capital Fireplaces Ltd is one of the UK's leading trade suppliers of cast iron fireplaces, stone fireplaces & marble fireplaces in the South of England. They are also one of the largest suppliers in the South of England of period and contemporary fireplaces, combining supreme craftsmanship, quality materials and elegance. Their latest innovations have focused on the need to reduce the running costs and adverse environmental impact of burning the variety of fuels that their products are suitable for.

Model: **Sirius 450 Glass**
Rated output kW: **4.5**
UK distributor: **Capital Fireplaces**
Address: **Unit 12-17 Henlow Trading Estate, Henlow Camp, Bedfordshire SG16 6DS**
Tel: **01462 813138**
Website: **capitalfireplaces.co.uk**

Model: **Sirius 600 Inset**
Rated output kW: **4.9**
UK distributor: **Capital Fireplaces**
Address: **Unit 12-17 Henlow Trading Estate, Henlow Camp, Bedfordshire SG16 6DS**
Tel: **01462 813138**
Website: **capitalfireplaces.co.uk**

# CHARLTON & JENRICK

Charlton & Jenrick Ltd are leading manufacturers and suppliers to the fireplace industry; through a number of carefully managed brands they supply local independent fireplace showrooms and high street retail chains. They have five industry leading brands covering all aspects and channels of the fireplace industry, which are; Paragon, Katell, Matchless, Fireline & Infinity Fires.

Model: **FPi5W**
Rated output kW: **4.9**
UK distributor: **Charlton & Jenrick**
Address: **Unit D Stafford Park 2, Telford, Shropshire, TF3 3AR**
Tel: **01952 200444**
Website: **www.charltonandJenrick. co.uk**

**HETAS**

# CHARNWOOD

AJ Wells produces stoves under the Charnwood name and manufactures all of its stoves in the UK. Their Tor range consists of three gently curved glass panels which offer a spectacular view of the fire from the front and from the sides whilst a highly advanced combustion system ensures exceptional clean burning and outstanding efficiency. There other ranges include Island, Cove, C Series and a range of boiler stoves.

Model: **Tor Pico**
Rated output kW: **5**
UK distributor: **AJ Wells & Sons**
Address: **Bishops Way, Newport
Isle of Wight, TF1 5AQ**
Tel: **+44 (0)1983 537777**
Website: **www.charnwood.com**

Model: **Cove 1**
Rated output kW: **4**
UK distributor: **AJ Wells & Sons**
Address: **Bishops Way, Newport
Isle of Wight, TF1 5AQ**
Tel: **+44 (0)1983 537777**
Website: **www.charnwood.com**

# CLEARVIEW

Clearview Stoves have been designed with exceptionally large and strong glass windows that give an excellent view of the fire. Unlike conventional stoves, the Clearview air distribution system means hours of clear fire viewing, without sooting or tarring of the stove windows. Clearview burns mixed fuels, or just coal, without detracting from the wood-burning efficiency. Clearview Smoke Control Stoves can be used in smoke control areas throughout the UK.

Model: **Pioneer 400**
Rated output kW: **5.0**
UK distributor: **Clearview Stoves**
Address: **More Works, Bishops Castle, Shropshire, SY9 5HH**
Tel: **01588 650401**
Website: **www.clearviewstoves.com**

**HETAS**

# DEMANICOR

De Manincor woodburning cooker stoves are high end stoves, elegantly designed with attention to aesthetics and function. One of the things which really set them apart is that many of the De Manincor wood cooker stoves can be combined with a matching gas/electric cooker which gives a unit that can provide practical, stylish cooking all year round.

Model: Atmosphera 900
Rated output kW: 11.0
UK distributor: Available from a number of UK distributors such as Ludlow Stoves Ltd
Address: Dickens Cottage, Culmington, Ludlow, Shropshire, SY8 2DB
Tel: 01584 861628
Website: www.ludlowstoves.co.uk

# DOVRE

Dovre's stoves and fireplaces are built in Scandanavia and are able to endure the harshest of Arctic winters. Dovre's manufacturing expertise with premium grade cast iron is such that all cast parts on their stoves and fireplaces come with a five year guarantee. There is a wide range to choose from and they manufacture traditional as well as contemporary styles. They also supply flue pipes and canopies.

Model: Vintage 35DV
Rated output kW: 8.0
UK distributor: Stovax Ltd,
Address: Falcon Road, Sowton
Industrial Estate, Exeter, Devon, EX2 7LF
Tel: 01392 474000
Website: www. dovre.co.uk

Model: Dovre Astroline 2CB
Rated output kW: 8.0
UK distributor: Stovax Ltd,
Address: Falcon Road, Sowton
Industrial Estate, Exeter, Devon, EX2 7LF
Tel: 01392 474000
Website: www. dovre.co.uk

# DOWLING

Dowling have been making stoves on a craft basis, working purely in heavy gauge steel, since 1983. Over that time they have evolved radically different designs from the norm, that have stood the test of time as well as performance. Their designs bring a variety and invention. They build by hand, in the heaviest gauges of steel used on the domestic stove market, that over the years have evolved into the seven basic models that they now offer; each radically different from anything else on the market, but each with a proven track record of performance, reliability and longevity.

Model: **Aztec**
Rated output kW: **6–25**
UK distributor: **Dowling Stoves**
Address: **Dowling, Unit 3, Bladnoch Bridge Estate, Newton Stewart, Scotland DG8 9AB**
Tel: **01988 402666**
Website: **www.dowlingstoves.com**

Model: **The Little Devil**
Rated output kW: **4-12**
UK distributor: **Dowling Stoves**
Address: **Dowling, Unit 3, Bladnoch Bridge Estate, Newton Stewart, Scotland DG8 9AB**
Tel: **01988 402666**
Website: **www.dowlingstoves.com**

# DROOF KAMINOFEN

Drooff Kaminöfen is located in Brilon, in the North Rhine-Westphalia region of Germany. The company was established in 1997 by Uwe Drooff and now produces over 7,500 contemporary wood burning stoves a year. The range is eye catching, engineered to be extremely efficient and manufactured to the highest standards warranting a five year guarantee. MMF Ltd is Drooff's exclusive distributor in the United Kingdom. MMF was established in 1975 and is a leading manufacturer and distributor to the stove dealer market. The company has six regional stocking branches and national sales representation.

Model: **Elba 4**
Rated output kW: **4.0**
UK distributor: **MMF Ltd**
Address: **Flue House, 55 Woodburn Road, Smethwick, West Midlands, B66 2PU**
Tel: **0121 5556555**
Website: **www.drooffstoves.com**

**Other models available**
Model: **Andalo**
Rated output kW: **4.0-8.0**

Model: **Aprica**
Rated output kW: **4.0–7.0**

Model: **Teglio**
Rated output kW: **4.0–7.0**

Model: **Varese 2**
Rated output kW: **8.0**

# DUNSLEY HEAT

Dunsley Heat are one of the UK's best manufacturers of high quality heating equipment including woodburning stoves. From providing heat and hot water for the whole house through the use of award winning multi-fuel stoves and wood burning stoves and back boilers, to providing the unique atmosphere only an open fire can create. They do not supply stoves or installation to the general public but will give you full details of the nearest stockist when contacted.

Model: **Highlander**
**Enviro-Burn 5**
Rated output kW: **4.9**
UK distributor: **Dunsley Heat Ltd**
Address: **Bridge Mills, Huddersfield Road, Holmfirth, Nr Huddersfield, West Yorkshire, HD9 3TW**
Tel: **01484 682635**
Website: **www.dunsleyheat.co.uk**

**HETAS**

Model: **Yorkshire**
Rated output kW: **13.7**
UK distributor: **Dunsley Heat Ltd**
Address: **Bridge Mills, Huddersfield Road, Holmfirth, Nr Huddersfield, West Yorkshire, HD9 3TW**
Tel: **01484 682635**
Website: **www.dunsleyheat.co.uk**

141

# ECCO

The Landy Vent Eccostove is an innovative new wood burning stove which is made of silicon carbide, and releases heat slowly, warming your entire home for hours at a time. Silicon Carbide is made up of two minerals extracted from the ground: Silicon and Carborundum. When combined, these minerals form one of the hardest materials on earth. Silicon Carbide is able to absorb extreme temperatures and then release heat slowly. It offers some of the best energy efficiencies and low levels of carbon available.

Model: **Ecco 850**
Rated output kW: **11.5**
(Wood)
UK distributor: **Landy Vent (UK) Ltd**
Address: **Foster House, 2 Redditch Road, Studley, Warwickshire, B80 7AX**
Tel: **01527 857814**
Website: **www. landyvent.co.uk**

**HETAS**

Model: **Ecco 678**
Rated output kW: **9.4**
(Wood)
UK distributor: **Landy Vent (UK) Ltd**
Address: **Foster House, 2 Redditch Road, Studley, Warwickshire, B80 7AX**
Tel: **01527 857814**
Website: **www. landyvent.co.uk**

**HETAS**

# ESSE ENGINEERING

ESSE is one of the UK's longest-standing stove manufacturer and produces cast iron range cookers, energy-efficient wood-burning stoves and stylish gas stoves. The knowledge and skills developed over more than a century and a half, go into everything they do and are hand built to last a lifetime. The wood burner stoves are highly efficient (up to 80%) and are fitted with Afterburn airwash technology for clear door glass and exceptional burn rate control.

Model: **100SE**
Rated output kW: **5.0**   **HETAS**
UK distributor: **Esse Engineering**
Address: **Long Ing, Barnoldswick,**
**Colne, Lancashire, B18 6BN**
Tel: **01282 813235**
Website: **www.esse.com**

# FONDIS

Fondis are based in Alsace, France, and specialise in making inset stoves. Fondis are pioneering when it comes to stove design: there are catalyst options to reduce emissions by around 90 per cent. They regularly use Visioceram glass which maintains a clear view of the fire. There are models available for airtight houses, and the door can slide up into the wall allowing the stove to be used like a fireplace.

**Model:** Stella 11 double sided
**Rated output kW:** 16
**UK distributor:** Firepower
**Address:** Units 11 & 12, Quadrant Distribution Centre, Quedgeley, Gloucester, GL2 2RN
**Tel:** 0845 8388758
**Website:** www. firepowerheating. co.uk

# FIREBELLY

Firebelly design and manufacture wood burning, multi fuel and gas stoves with the latest technology and combined with time honoured and beautiful designs to offer customers everything they would want from a contemporary stove. They can provide assistance from start to finish, helping choose the right stove and ensuring it performs through the years with maintenance advice and spares. They also offer an installation service.

Model: **Firebelly FB**
Rated output kW: **5.0**
UK distributor: **Firebelly Stoves**
Address: **Unit C Ainleys Industrial Estate, Elland, HX5 9JP**
Tel: **01422 375582**
Website: **www. firebellystoves.com**

Model: **Firepod**
Rated output kW: **10.0**
UK distributor: **Firebelly Stoves**
Address: **Unit C Ainleys Industrial Estate, Elland, HX5 9JP**
Tel: **01422 375582**
Website: **www. firebellystoves.com**

# FRANCO BELGE

Franco Belge has a history spanning 80 years. Their brand name is synonymous with heritage, quality castings and beautiful period designs. The product range contains wood, multifuel, gas and oil stoves. The appliances have a heat output from 4.5 kW up to 11 kW. ACR do not deal with the public directly and you will need to contact them to locate details of their dealer network.

Model: Montfort Classic Ivory
Rated output kW: 5.0
UK distributor: ACR Heat Products
Address: Unit 1, Weston Works,
Weston Lane, Tyseley, Birmingham,
B11 3RP
Tel: 0121 7068266
Website: www.acrheatproducts.
co.uk

# HARRIE LEENDERS

Harrie Leenders has been setting the standard in Holland for 25 years. The founder and name of the firm has carved a reputation for innovation and perfectionism. His ideal was written in fire: to make user-friendly stoves with almost 100% combustion. All models follow this idea and the unique combustion chambers in these stoves reduces emissions.

Model: **Fuga M**
Rated output kW: **10.0**
UK distributor: **Robeys Ltd**
Address: **Goods Road, Belper,**
**Derbyshire, DE56 1UU**
Tel: **01773 820940**
Website: **www.robeys.co.uk**

HETAS

Model: **Fuga eL**
Rated output kW: **8.5**
UK distributor: **Robeys Ltd**
Address: **Goods Road, Belper,**
**Derbyshire, DE56 1UU**
Tel: **01773 820940**
Website: **www.robeys.co.uk**

HETAS

147

# HASE-KAMINOFENBAU

Hase woodburning stoves have been handmade in Germany since 1979 in their factory in Trier. Made completely from steel or in soapstone or ceramic versions – every stove model has its own distinctive character. In UK they are represented by Anglia Fireplaces Ltd.

Model: **Lima**
Rated output kW: **6.0**
UK distributor: **Anglia Fireplaces**
Address: **Anglia House, Kendal Court, Cambridge Road, Impington, Cambridge, CB24 9YS**
Tel: **01223 234713**
Website: **www.fireplaces.co.uk**

# HEAT DESIGN

Heat Design specialise in many types of cast iron stoves including wood burning stoves, multi fuel stoves, contemporary stoves, gas stoves and electric stoves. Heat Design also stock a full range of stove accessories. Complementing a traditional or contemporary look in any home, a cast iron stove is the perfect solution to efficient heating with the ambience of a real fire.

Model: TR Steel
Rated output kW: 5.00
UK distributor: Heat Design
Address: 60 Hawthorn Road,
Western Industrial Estate, Naas
Road, Dublin 12, Republic of
Ireland
Tel: +(00) 353 14089192
Website: www. tripp.ie

# HOTPOD

Hotpod is an expanding range of contemporary multi fuel and wood burning stoves and accessories, designed and hand built in St. Ives in the far west of Cornwall, from recycled materials. Created by artist blacksmith Daniel Harding and influenced by the Cornish environment and surf culture, the award winning Hotpod are now Defra exempt appliances for use in smoke free zones.

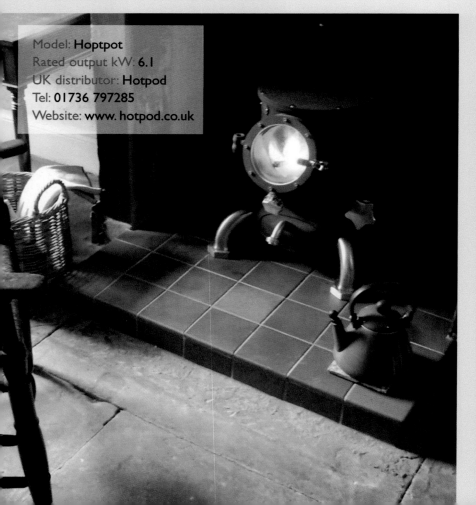

Model: **Hoptpot**
Rated output kW: **6.1**
UK distributor: **Hotpod**
Tel: **01736 797285**
Website: **www. hotpod.co.uk**

# HUNTER

Based in Devon, Hunter have been making stoves for around 40 years. They make a range of traditionally styled, yet unfussy, multifuel and woodburning stoves. Most Hunter stoves can come with either double or single doors, and a wide range of boiler models are also available. They also use Cleanburn, a system that significantly reduces the carbon emissions from a traditional stove.

Model: **Kestrel 5**
Rated output kW: **4.6**
UK distributor: **Hunter Stoves Ltd,**
Address: **Aspen House, Pynes Hill,**
**Exeter, Devon, EX2 5AZ**
Tel: **01392 422760**
Website: **www.hunterstoves.co.uk**

Model: **Nørreskoven**
Rated output kW: **4.4**
UK distributor: **Hunter Stoves Ltd,**
Address: **Aspen House, Pynes Hill,**
**Exeter, Devon, EX2 5AZ**
Tel: **01392 422760**
Website: **www.hunterstoves.co.uk**

# JACOBUS

Ever since 1981, Jacobus wood-burning stoves have been designed and produced in Janco de Jong's iron-work atelier in Gorredijk, Holland. An important advantage for the user is that the glass of the stove stays perfectly clean as the combustion is cleaner. Moreover, the Jacobus also offers the option to add outside air which makes the stove ideal for using it in insulated (newly built) homes.

Model: Jacobus 6
Rated output kW: 7.0
UK distributor: Landy Vent (UK) Ltd
Address: Foster House, 2 Redditch Road, Studley, Warwickshire, B80 7AX
Tel: 01527 857814
Website: www. landyvent.co.uk

**Other stoves available**
Model: Jacobus 9.0
Rated output kW: 10.0

Model: Jacobus 12
Rated output kW: 14.0

# JETMASTER

Jetmaster make wood-burning open fires, wood stoves and multi fuel stoves of distinction. Jetmaster stove fireplaces are designed to burn multi-fuel. With their multi-fuel basket you can choose the fuel that's right for you — whether you burn logs, a coal and wood mix, turf/peat, briquettes or other smokeless fuels — burn multi-fuel when you use a basket grate.

Model: **Jetmaster 18f**
Rated output kW: **4.9**
UK distributor: **Jetmaster Fires**
Address: **Unit 2, Peacock Trading Centre, Goodwood Road, Eastleigh, Hampshire, SO50 4NT**
Tel: **012380 629513**
Website: **www.jetmaster.co.uk**

Model: **Jetmaster 60 Inset**
Rated output kW: **4.9**
UK distributor: **Jetmaster Fires**
Address: **Unit 2, Peacock Trading Centre, Goodwood Road, Eastleigh, Hampshire, SO50 4NT**
Tel: **012380 629513**
Website: **www.jetmaster.co.uk**

153

# JØTUL

Jøtul has one of the world's biggest and most experienced network of dealers and have produced fireplaces from cast iron since 1853. They have a very wide range of stoves and were one of the first stove importers into this country. Their stoves have never been cheap but have always been known for their high quality, good looks and very efficient wood burning. To find your local dealer go to **www.jotul.com**

Model: **F162**
Rated output kW: **5.0**
UK distributor: **Jøtul stoves are available from a large number of retailers including Norflame**
Address: **Notcutts Garden Centre, Daniels Road, Norwich, NR4 6QP**
Tel: **01603 505575**
Website: **www.norflame.co.uk**

Model: **F371**
Rated output kW: **5.5**
UK distributor: **Jøtul stoves are available from a large number of retailers includingThe Hot Spot**
Address: **Dovefields, Uttoxeter Staffordshire ST14 8GA**
Tel: **01889 565411**
Website: **thehotspot.co.uk**

# MENDIP

Mendip Stoves are manufacturers of high quality, well designed, wood burning and multi fuel stoves with a wide range covering traditional and contemporary stylings. There is something to suit every taste. They have been designing and producing wood burning and multi fuel stoves of the highest quality, and have developed a reputation for supplying only stoves with the best combustion techniques, looks and build quality.

Model: **Mendip 5SE**
Rated output kW: **4.8**
UK distributor: **Mendip Stoves Ltd**
Address: **Unit S5, Mendip Industrial Estate, Mendip Road, Somerset, BS26 2UG**
Tel: **01934 750500**
Website: **www.mendipstoves.co.uk**

**Other models available**
Model: **Mendip 8**
Rated output kW: **8.3**

Model: **Loxton Series**
Rated output kW: **3.2–8.0**

Model: **Churchill Series**
Rated output kW: **5.0–10.0**

Model: **Somerton**
Rated output kW: **7.0**

# MORSØ UK

Morsø have been making cast-iron wood burning stoves for more than 150 years. They hand-pick their dealers not only for their intimate knowledge of wood burning stoves, but for their customer service too. They will help you choose the right wood burner for your home, fit it, and care for it over the years to come. They offer a wide range including wall-hanging, inserts, Defra approved and free standing.

Model: **6140**
Rated output kW: **5.0**
UK distributor: **Morsø UK Ltd**
Address: **Unit 7, The io Centre,**
**Valley Drive, Swift Valley, Rugby,**
**Warwickshire, CV21 1TW**
Tel: **01788 554410**
Website: **www.morsoe.com**

Model: **Panther 2110**
Rated output kW: **9.0**
UK distributor: **Morsø UK Ltd**
Address: **Unit 7, The io Centre,**
**Valley Drive, Swift Valley, Rugby,**
**Warwickshire, CV21 1TW**
Tel: **01788 554410**
Website: **www.morsoe.com**

▶ A Morsø 6140

# NIBE (CONTURA)

Contura wood burning stoves are available in a number of variants and are extremely well designed. Several of the stoves are available in at least two colours, grey and black. Most of the stoves have really generous glass areas on three sides. The stoves have very efficient fireboxes with an efficiency of up to 81 % which is one of the highest on the market according to independent testers.

Model: **Contura 470**
Rated output kW: **7.0**   **HETAS**
UK distributor: **Contura stoves are available from a number of retailers including Corinium Stoves**
Address: **Unit 14 Elliott Road Love Lane Ind. Est. Cirencester, Gloucestershire. GL7 1YS**
Tel: **01285 659887**
Website: **www. corinium-stoves. co.uk**

Model: **Contura 590T**
Rated output kW: **5.0**  **HETAS**
UK distributor: **Contura stoves are available from a number of retailers including Corinium Stoves**
Address: **Unit 14 Elliott Road Love Lane Ind. Est. Cirencester, Gloucestershire. GL7 1YS**
Tel: **01285 659887**
Website: **www. corinium-stoves. co.ukco.uk**

# portway

## STOVES

##  **high**efficiency

## Clean, efficient & built to last.

Portway multifuel, wood, and gas stoves burn slower to gain the maximum heat from your fuel.

Choose from contemporary or traditional designs with built in technology for efficiences up to 75%+.

**10** YEAR GUARANTEE

MADE IN BRITAIN

## www.portway-stoves.co.uk

Call: 01782 339000   Email: info@bfm-europe.com

NOVA SUPRA EUROPA SMW IL ILS SIGMA SELFLEX

# SFL
### flues & chimneys
## Solutions For Life

NOVA System:

The complete solution for Solid Fuel, Condensing, Biomass, Wood-Chip & Pellet Appliances

Nova is the most versatile chimney system on the market, offering a single solution for virtually all of today's combustion requirements. Nova is a true multi-fuel / multi-application product, whether being used to serve a solid fuel stove, vent the latest high efficiency condensing appliances or Biomass wood chip / pellet stove, Nova is the product of choice. Nova is built to last and is designed with a rapid fit multi-barbed twist lock jointing system.

Other systems that complement the NOVA range include SELFLEX and SIGMA

To view our full range of systems for every application, domestic or large-scale, visit our website or contact Customer Service on 01271 326633 for further information and to find a distributor in your area.

## 100% British Manufacturing

## www.sflchimneys.com

# NORDICA EXTRAFLAME

La Nordica are a leading Italian manufacturer of stoves who make a wide range of inset, freestanding and range cooker stoves with and without boilers, some of which are Defra Exempt for use in smoke control areas. Extraflame switched to designing, developing and producing pellet stoves which are environmentally friendly products and have firmly established the company as one of today's market leaders.

Model: **Emma Plus**
Rated output kW: **3.6–11.0**
UK distributor: **La Nordica stoves are available from a number of retailers including Stovesonline**
Address: **Capton, Dartmouth, Devon, TQ6 0JE**
Tel: **0845 226 5754**

# NORDPEIS

Nordpeis is a Norwegian company founded over 20 years ago and produces a diverse range of wood burning stoves to a suit a variety of homes. With the latest Cleanburn and Airwash technology, these highly efficient wood burning stoves can be enjoyed either from the corner of your home or placed in a cosy inglenook. The Quadro 2 stove pictured below gives a wide view of the fire and is ideal for installation in the corner of a room.

Model: **Nordpeis Quadro 2**
Rated output kW: **6.2**
UK distributor: **Nordpeis stoves are available from a number of retailers including Nonfumo Flue Systems**
Address: **West House, Slough Lane Saunderton, High Wycombe, Bucks, HP14 4HN**
Tel: **01494 565361**
Website: **www.fluesystems.com**

# PANADERO

Panadero have been manufacturing high quality designer stoves for over 60 years in the south east of Spain. They use advanced CNC technology and teamed with their vast production capacity, unbeatable logistics and efficiency demonstrates why they are extremely popular throughout Europe. The stoves are guaranteed for two years and they offer contemporary, traditional and vertical options.

Model: **Boston**
Rated output kW: **9.5**
UK distributor: **The Marble Warehouse**
Address: **Maritime Industrial Estate Maesycoed, Pontypridd, CF37 1NY**
Tel: **01443 408548**
Website: **www.panaderostoves.com**

Model: **Sierra**
Rated output kW: **8.9**
UK distributor: **The Marble Warehouse**
Address: **Maritime Industrial Estate Maesycoed, Pontypridd, CF37 1NY**
Tel: **01443 408548**
Website: **www.panaderostoves.com**

# PARKRAY

Parkray has been producing heating components since 1850. Originally known as 'Park Foundry', the company quickly become the leading name in solid fuel appliances. Today, Parkray is based near Exeter in Devon on the same site as Hunter Stoves (see page 153). They are still developing innovative features for solid fuel heating and still building every stove to the highest standards.

Model: **Compact 5**
Rated output kW: **4.5**
UK distributor: **Parkray Ltd,**
Address: **Aspen House, Pynes Hill,**
**Exeter, Devon, EX2 5AZ**
Tel: **01392 422760**
Website: **www.hunterstoves.co.uk**

Model: **Derwent 5**
Rated output kW: **4.6**
UK distributor: **Parkray Ltd,**
Address: **Aspen House, Pynes Hill,**
**Exeter, Devon, EX2 5AZ**
Tel: **01392 422760**
Website: **www.hunterstoves.co.uk**

# PERCY DOUGHTY

Percy Doughty & Co. are on of the biggest wholesale suppliers of fireplaces in the UK and pride themselves on their ability to supply quality products with a great service at a fantastic price. They have huge stocks of fireplaces, stoves, solid fuel spares and accessories and sell a large range of woodburning stoves including Charnwood, and Kooga.

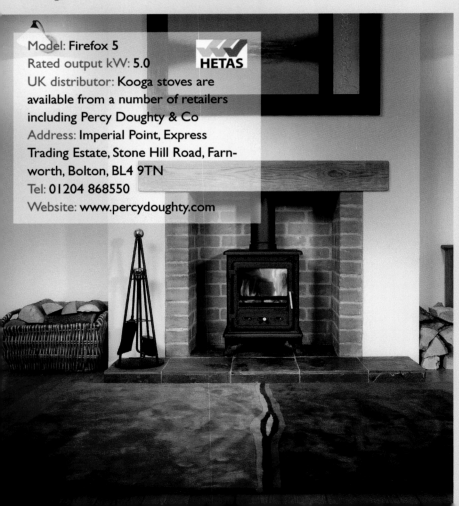

Model: Firefox 5
Rated output kW: 5.0
UK distributor: Kooga stoves are available from a number of retailers including Percy Doughty & Co
Address: Imperial Point, Express Trading Estate, Stone Hill Road, Farnworth, Bolton, BL4 9TN
Tel: 01204 868550
Website: www.percydoughty.com

HETAS

# PEVEX ENTERPRISES

Pevex Enterprises was established in 1993 as importers and distributors of traditional fire baskets, grates, and fire backs to the fireplace industry. As the business has developed, fireplaces were added to the product range and were successfully sold to their retail network. There sell a variety of stoves including Bohemia, Serenity inset stoves, Suffolk traditional stoves and Heta stoves from Denmark.

Model: **Bohemia X30**
Rated output kW: **3**
UK distributor: **Pevex Enterprises**
Address: **Unit 12F Seven Acres Business Park, Newbourne Road, Waldringfield, Nr Woodbridge, Suffolk IP12 4PS**
Tel: **01473 736399**
Website: **www.woodstoves.co.uk**

# ROBEYS

At Robeys they have a vast range of contemporary stoves that will 'fuel' your imagination. Their diverse collection includes the popular Clearview stoves, Harrie Leenders ceiling mounted rotatable stoves, Piazzetta double and triple sided stoves and the elegant Rais stoves range. All of their stoves are renowned for their style, functionality and exceptional quality and use cutting edge technology for fuel efficiency and are Defra approved.

Model: **Rais Q-bic**
Rated output kW: **4.5** **HETAS**
UK distributor: **Robeys Ltd**
Address: **Goods Road, Belper, Derbyshire, DE56 1UU**
Tel: **01773 820940**
Website: **www.robeys.co.uk**

# PYROCLASSIC FIRES

Pyroclassic Fires began making stoves over 30 years ago in New Zealand and although the original principles of the Pyroclassic Fire like the cylindrical ceramic fire chamber have remained unchanged since the very beginning there have been numerous minor improvements. Fundementally, the Pyroclassic IV is a heat store. With over 40 kgs of ceramic heat storage capacity it has the ability to recover masses of excess heat generated by a hot, bright fire inside its thick cylindrical fire chamber, and it is this heat storage capacity that gives the Pyroclassic IV its ability to release heat throughout the night.

Model: **Pyroclassic IV**
Rated output kW: **5.0**
UK distributor: **Pyroclassic Fires Ltd**
Address: **72 Hill Top Avenue**
**Cheadle Hulme, Cheshire, SK8 7JA**
Tel: **07712 400252**
Website: **www.pyroclassic.co.uk**

# RIKA

This family run company has become a leading stove producer since its foundation 60 years ago and is today synonymous with the most innovative products of excellent quality. All products are guaranteed and made in Austria. Improving the tried and trusted and developing new products – this is how RIKA presents itself as the leading producer of woodburning and pellet stoves. A woodburning or pellet stove from Rika combines innovation and easy operation in maximum combustion efficiency and very good design.

Model: **Scena**
Rated output kW: **10**   **HETAS**
UK distributor: **Euroheat Ltd**
Address: **Court Farm Business Park,
Bishops Frome, Worcestershire,
WR6 5AY**
Tel: **01885 4951100**
Website: **www.euroheat.co.uk**

Model: **Vetra**
Rated output kW: **4.0**  **HETAS**
UK distributor: **Euroheat Ltd**
Address: **Court Farm Business Park,
Bishops Frome, Worcestershire,
WR6 5AY**
Tel: **01885 4951100**
Website: **www.euroheat.co.uk**

# ROFER AND RODI

Rofer & Rodi's activity centres on the manufacture of fireplaces and barbecues, bringing together broad experience and innovation. Their products are the result of technological development and know-how, using the best raw materials and the most dedicated designs. All this makes it possible for them to offer a wide range of fireplaces of the best quality.

Model: **Onuba**
Rated output kW: **7.0**
UK distributor: **Rofer and Rodi**
Address: **Unit 10, Airedale Business Centre, Millenium Road, Skipton, North Yorkshire, BD32 2TZ**
Tel: **01756 700004**
Website: **www.rofer.co.uk**

Model: **Iliberis**
Rated output kW: **7.0**
UK distributor: **Rofer and Rodi**
Address: **Unit 10, Airedale Business Centre, Millenium Road, Skipton, North Yorkshire, BD32 2TZ**
Tel: **01756 700004**
Website: **www.rofer.co.uk**

# SALAMANDER

Salamader stoves are a Devon based company that is dedicated to providing personal, attentive service in the wholesale supply, installation and manufacture of high quality cast iron multi fuel stoves. They recognised that there was a demand for a quality cast iron stove which had a smaller footprint to other stoves on the market. The Hobbit was the result and it is suitable where the space for a stove is more limited.

Model: **Hobbit**
Rated output kW: **4**
UK distributor: **Salamander Stoves**
Address: **Rosemount, Canada Hill, Ogwell, Devon, TQ12 6AF**
Tel: **01626 363507**
Website: **www.salamanderstoves. com**

**Other stoves available**
Model: **Pipsqueak**
Rated output kW: **3.0**

# STOVAX

Based at Exeter, Stovax Ltd was established in 1981 to design, manufacture and distribute wood burning stoves and fireside accessories. In 2006 they acquired Yeoman stoves which has continued under its own brand name. Stovax through its sister company Gazco distribute Wamsler solid fuel cookers and stoves. Today the Stovax group is the UK's largest stove and fireplace producer.

Model: **Riva Plus Midi**
Rated output kW: **6.5**
UK distributor: **Stovax Ltd**
Address: **Falcon Road, Sowton Industrial Esate, Exeter, Devon, EX2 7LF**
Tel: **01392 474000**
Website: **www.stovax.com**

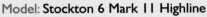

Model: **Stockton 6 Mark 11 Highline**
Rated output kW: **6.0**
UK distributor: **Stovax Ltd**
Address: **Falcon Road, Sowton Industrial Esate, Exeter, Devon, EX2 7LF**
Tel: **01392 474000**
Website: **www.stovax.com**

173

# TERMATECH

Termatech stoves are wood burning appliances which appeal to home owners who are concerned about the rising cost of gas and electricity. The Termatech stoves have a cast iron base and door, ensuring any parts of the stove that come into direct contact with the fire are robust and able to cope with the rigours of the combustion process. With a large glass door there is a great view of the fire. Designed with the latest air wash technology the glass remains clear during the burning process and the view of the fire remains uninterrupted. The appliance has a stay cool handle allowing the user to open the stove to reload without the use of gloves.

Model: TermaTech 20RS
Rated output kW: 5.0
UK distributor: Specflue
Address: 8 Curzon Road, Chilton Industrial Estate, Sudbury, Suffolk CO10 2XW
Tel: 0800 9020220

# VARDE

Varde Ovne are Danish contemporary stoves produced by Varde and have been manufactured since 1987 in Jutland, Denmark. The contemporary plain design combined with high efficiency ratings have made them popular in Europe. All the models are convection stoves and have quite a few features that make them an attractive choice. The cast iron top and doors gives a sturdy appearance and the fact that all exposed parts are forged in cast iron gives a very good build quality. The glass has an air wash system which helps to keep the glass clean and the handle is tempered and therefore cool to touch when re-loading fuel.

Model: **Aura 1**
Rated output kW: **5.0**
UK distributor: **Nordpeis stoves are available from a number of retailers including Nonfumo Flue Systems**
Address: **West House, Slough Lane Saunderton, High Wycombe, Bucks, HP14 4HN**
Tel: **01494 565361**
Website: **www.fluesystems.com**

# VERMONT CASTINGS

Vermont Castings are a company based in the heart of Vermont, USA, where the traditions of hearth and home have stood the test of time. For over 35 years, Vermont Castings has been committed to providing stoves with iconic style and superior heating efficiency. They are one of the few manufacturers to use catalysts and from their green manufacturing process to Environmental Protection Agency (EPA) certified models, the company is very 'green' in its manufacturing. All stoves are made from recycled iron and other reused raw materials.

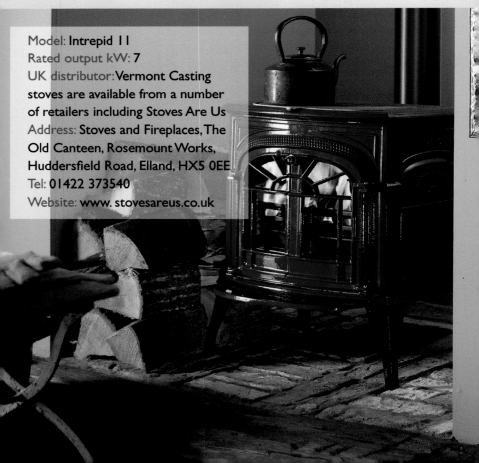

Model: **Intrepid 11**
Rated output kW: **7**
UK distributor: **Vermont Casting stoves are available from a number of retailers including Stoves Are Us**
Address: **Stoves and Fireplaces, The Old Canteen, Rosemount Works, Huddersfield Road, Elland, HX5 0EE**
Tel: **01422 373540**
Website: **www. stovesareus.co.uk**

# WATERFORD STANLEY

Waterford Stanley are an Irish company with a long and proud tradition, and have been bringing warmth and comfort to homes for generations, stretching back to when the first range cooker which was made in Waterford in 1934. They produce a wide range of wood burning stoves from room heaters to the Donard which is a cooker with boiler and can power up to 12 radiators.

Model: **Donard**
Rated output kW: **17.6**
UK distributor: **Waterford Stanley stoves are available from a number of retailers including Woodstock Fires**
Address: **Heathfield, East Sussex TN21 8LD**
Tel: **01435 868686**
Website: **www. woodstockfires. co.uk**

Waterford Stanley also produce a range of wood burning stoves and some models are available with boilers.
Model: **Erin**
Rated output kW: **14.7**

Model: **Ardmore with boiler**
Rated output kW: **3.5 to room and 8.5 to water.**

# WESTFIRE

Westfire is a Danish company situated in Jutland. The Danes are used to severely cold winters and therefore have developed the art of constructing functional and stylish wood burners to see them through the seasons. They have concentrated on contemporary designs with the sort of functionality you need in a modern new build property such as smaller nominal outputs and direct air supply.

Model: Westfire 1
Rated output kW: **4.9**
UK distributor: **Westfire stoves are available from a number of retailers including Stovesonline**
Address: **Capton, Dartmouth, Devon, TQ6 0JE**
Tel: **0845 226 5754**
Website: **www. stovesonline.co.uk**

# WOODFIRE

Woodfire boiler stoves are designed to burn wood at high efficiencies and can connect directly into pressurised, or open vented systems. A variety of models are available ranging from 12 to 24kW heat output: the robust RS inset stoves (which includes double sided versions), the more modern Nx inset stoves and the freestanding Firo.

Model: **RS19**
Rated output kW: **16.7 to water and 2.3 to room**
UK distributor: **Westfire stoves are available from a number of retailers including Stovesonline**
Address: **Capton, Dartmouth, Devon, TQ6 OJE**
Tel: **0845 226 5754**
Website: **www. stovesonline.co.uk**

# WOODWARM

All Woodwarm stoves feature an excellent air wash system. After circulating the stove, pre-heated air flushes down over the double glazed door keeping the glass perfectly clean at all times, even at low temperatures. Superior clean burn efficiency means that not only is more heat achieved on less fuel, but combustion products in the flue are also reduced, causing fewer flue problems. Reduction in pollution combined with more efficiency creates a more environmentally friendly device.

Model: **The Fireview double depth**
Rated output kW: **9.0**
UK distributor: **Woodwarm Stoves**
Address: **Metal Developments Ltd.
The Workshop, Wheatcroft Farm,
Cullompton, Devon EX15 1RA**
Tel: **01884 35806**
Website: **www. woodwarmstoves.
co.uk**

# Appendix

The installation of a stove requires an expert and we highly recommend that you do not install a stove yourself. HETAS are the official body recognised by the government to approve biomass and solid fuel domestic heating appliances, fuels and services including the registration of competent installers and servicing businesses and their website and other useful websites are detailed below.

Association of Plumbing and Heating Contractors
**www.aphc.co.uk**
British Flue and Chimney Manufactuers Association
**www.bfcma.co.uk**
Building Engineering Services Competence Assessement (BESCA)
**www.besca.org.uk**
Defra (The Department for Environment and Rural Affairs
**www.gov.uk/defra**
Find out if you live in a smoke controlled area
**www.smokecontrol.defra.gov.uk**
Forestry Commission
**www.forestresearch.gov.uk/fr/woodfuel**
For installation expertise
**www.hetas.co.uk**
Guild of Master Chimney Sweeps
**www. guildofmasterchimneysweeps.co.uk**
National Association for Professional Inspectors and Testers (NAPIT)
**www.napit.org.uk**
National Inspection Council for Electrical Installation Contracting (NICEIC)
**www.niceic.com**
Small Woods Association
**www.smallwoods.org.uk**
Stove Industry Alliance
**www.stoveindustryalliance.com**
Stove reviews
**www.whatstove.co.uk**
§The Forest Stewardship Council
**www.fsc-uk.org**
The Green deal scheme
**www.energysavingtrust.org.uk**
Woodland Management
**www.sylva.org.uk/myforest**

# Firing Imaginations for over 30 years...

## STOVAX
*Fire Your Imagination*

 Over 30 years of British design and engineering have gone into creating the UK's most comprehensive range of high quality wood and solid-fuel stoves & fireplaces

HIGH EFFICIENCY  •  ENVIRONMENTALLY FRIENDLY  •  TECHNICAL INNOVATION

www.stovax.com  •  0844 4141 322

# Index